# HOW YOUR CHILDREN CAN LEARN
## TO LIVE A REWARDING LIFE

# How Your Children Can Learn To Live a Rewarding Life

## Behavior Modification For Parents and Teachers

**ALEXANDER BANNATYNE, Ph.D.**

*Director, Bannatyne Children's Learning Center*
*Miami, Florida*

*Formerly*
*Member, Center for Advanced Practice*
*Adler Zone Center, Illinois*
*Associate Professor of Special Education*
*Institute for Research on Exceptional Children*
*Director, Learning Disabilities Research Project*
*Children's Research Center*
*University of Illinois*
*Urbana, Illinois*

**MARYL BANNATYNE, M.A.**

*Co-Director, Bannatyne Children's Learning Center*
*Miami, Florida*

**CHARLES C THOMAS • PUBLISHER**
*Springfield • Illinois • U.S.A.*

*Published and Distributed Throughout the World by*
CHARLES C THOMAS • PUBLISHER
BANNERSTONE HOUSE
301-327 East Lawrence Avenue, Springfield, Illinois, U.S.A.

ISBN 0-398-02572-X
©*1973, by* CHARLES C THOMAS • PUBLISHER
Library of Congress Catalog Card Number: 72-81669

*With* THOMAS BOOKS *careful attention is given to all details of
manufacturing and design. It is the Publisher's desire to present books
that are satisfactory as to their physical qualities and artistic possibilities
and appropriate for their particular use.* THOMAS BOOKS *will be true
to those laws of quality that assure a good name and good will.*

*Printed in the United States of America*
*A-2*

*for*
**LYNNE**
**ROBIN**
and
**KATE**

# PREFACE

FOR SEVERAL YEARS NOW, psychologists have been developing some completely new techniques of child rearing—techniques of which many parents, teachers, and students are unaware. These new methods of bringing up children are collectively called "behavior modification," and it is the purpose of this book to bring to intelligent parents, teachers, and students a detailed summary of the nature and practice of behavior modification as applied to children in all types of situations in the home and classroom.

Unlike many of the old ideas about child rearing, behavior-modification techniques are founded in sound psychological theory, and even more important, they have a wealth of published research proof to demonstrate that they really do work. Traditionally, many parents and teachers, in desperation, have had to fall back on the rather negative methods of physical punishment, nagging, sarcasm, angry "telling off," and the withdrawal of love and affection.

This book presents the necessary background information and concrete practical plans for bringing up children in a way which is largely positive and constructive. The format of the book is unusual. Because for most readers the subject matter is so new, much of the text takes the form of paragraphs which are explanations of the specific words and phrases you will need to understand. This is a very easy and enjoyable way to learn, especially when the explanations are copiously laced with practical everyday examples of these new behavior modification techniques at work.

If you are responsible for bringing up or teaching children of any age, for the sake of those children it is extremely important that you become competent in the new techniques of behavior modification.

ALEXANDER AND MARYL BANNATYNE

# CONTENTS

## Contents

# HOW YOUR CHILDREN CAN LEARN
# TO LIVE A REWARDING LIFE

*Chapter I*

# INTRODUCTION

T HE TERMS BEHAVIOR MODIFICATION, reinforcement therapy, behavioral management, and many others are frequently heard or read these days in colleges, schools, and even in rare popular articles. People often use these terms, and the principles they involve, very loosely. Therefore, one of our first aims is to explain and define clearly all the technical words you are likely to come across either in books on the subject or in conversation with behavioral psychologists and educators. Our second objective is to describe in some detail with examples how you can successfully manage the positive and negative behaviors that children have.

Most important of all are the lists of positive behaviors which we think most people would consider to be desirable facets of their children's personalities. The way in which these positive behaviors can be thoroughly learned by growing children is described. It may surprise some people that children have to *learn* how to be creative, friendly, studious, responsible, considerate of others, and industrious, and how to enjoy themselves, to be resourceful, and generally to live a rich and rewarding life—one which benefits not only themselves but those around them. Naturally, it would take many volumes to describe in detail the tremendous psychological and social complexity necessary to a full understanding of how to build in children all the positive behaviors just listed. Therefore, it is incumbent on the parent or teacher to be somewhat independently creative themselves as they come to understand and implement the programs provided in later sections. This can best be accomplished by carefully studying and thinking about the definitions and principles which follow. Note that there are two kinds of learning.

We can learn to rote memorize automatic formulas or we can

learn the principles on which they work. Unfortunately, most people prefer the recipe-book rote memory system, which is the least effective technique. Once we learn the *principles* of how any aspect of life operates (including our own lives) we have an immense mastery and control over our environment. Principles allow us to tailor-make our own tactics, techniques, and handling procedures on the spot in order to control or manage a specific situation.

In working with parents and teachers, we have had several failures because sometimes the *adult* in charge of the children in question is incapable of slightly modifying or adapting his own personality to the principles of the management program. Children live in an environment and they look to the adult in that environment for management. It is well known that only by modifying the daily, child-management environment (and of course the most important aspect of that environment is the adult) that the behavior of children can be modified. Thus, if a parent or teacher wishes to have his children behave differently, he himself must examine his own behavior first. One mother came to us with a little boy of four years who had violent temper tantrums. After some probing, the mother admitted that her method of controlling the children was mostly one of "screaming and shouting" at them. In other words, she herself threw temper tantrums, and therefore it was not surprising that her youngest child had imitated her very efficiently, an example of "accidental training." A detailed program of behavior modification was prescribed which would extinguish the temper tantrums in the child. After two or three weeks it was found that even with supervision, the mother was quite incapable of controlling her own displays of verbal aggression and so the reinforcement therapy failed. The answer to that situation was to place the *mother* on a temper tantrum extinction program, but this was so threatening to her established life pattern of behaving that she withdrew before any real progress could be made.

Any effort by parents or teachers to adapt their own behavior to creative management programs for children will be rewarded many times over. There is one more important point to make. It is now known that if anyone wishes to shape, extinguish, build, or modify any behavior, the program must be in operation all waking hours of the day. This is the reason why the "behavior therapist" likes to work with, and through, the parent and teacher. Let us assume that a child in need of help came to a clinic for one hour a day for behavior shaping, while for all the other hours of the day in the home and at school, the child carried on with his negative or "maladaptive" behavior. It is obvious that the child's problems will be in no way changed. Many parents endow the behavior therapist with a magician's mantle and imagine that a miraculous transformation will take place in their child over a few short sessions. When they discover that not only is this not the case, but that they themselves must carry through the pre-scribed program, they are dismayed. However, there is no other way. The parent and teacher *must intervene* in the family relation-ships and follow through a daily program if the behavior of a member of that family is to change radically. No one else can do it for you. The results for parent and teacher are well worth the effort. In fact, the time saved in the long run, the human misery which is eliminated, and the general well-being of the family, make the fulfilling of a behavioral-management program worth every minute spent on it.

As will be seen, the great contribution which behavior modifica-tion has made to learning theory and child rearing is to redirect the emphasis toward rewarding (reinforcing) *positive behaviors* in order to establish them and deemphasize punishing negative behaviors. This *change of emphasis* to positive or constructive be-haviors and away from negative or nonconstructive behaviors is not fully appreciated even by many psychologists and educators who use and teach operant reinforcement techniques. Thus, it is not the principles of behavior modification which are new. What is new is the "discovery" that immediately rewarding *virtuous be-havior* will neither spoil the child nor cause him to rest on his laurels. He will not become swellheaded. What *does* happen is that he delevops a worthy concept of himself as a successful, fulfilled person who goes cheerfuly to work, happily secure in the knowl-edge that his efforts will be appreciated.

One more important point about the book must be made before we proceed to the definitions and explanations in Chapter II. In subjects such as psychology and education, the really interesting discussions, examples, and information have to wait for the last half of the book, whereas the first half is taken up with explaining terms and principles. This is unavoidable. The authors recommend that many readers delve into Chapter VI right now, because the experience should motivate them to return to Chapter II and read the more fundamental material which forms the basis of a sounder understanding of this relatively new approach to child rearing.

*Chapter II*

# GENERAL
# DEFINITIONS AND EXPLANATIONS

I N THE FOLLOWING DEFINITIONS and explanations of the terminology used in behavior modification, some terms unavoidably have to be used in definitions before they themselves have been defined. Therefore, it may be necessary occasionally to "jump around" from term to term in order to understand fully the psychological processes involved. An efficient way might be to read the chapter twice, the first time to get an overall picture and the second time for a more thorough study of what is involved.

*Behavior*

Any act, action, or response which has an effect on the individual and/or his environment is called a behavior. For all practical purposes, a behavior must be *observable* if it is to be modified in some way. If a behavior is to be modified, the intervener (the person doing the modifying) must be able to *recognize* a particular behavior, *discriminate* it from other behaviors, and *isolate* it in terms of its activity. This is most important, as no one wishes to modify behaviors at random or, to use a dental analogy, "pull the wrong tooth."

Examples of various behaviors are listed below.

| *Positive Behavior* | *Negative Behavior* |
|---|---|
| kind | unkind |
| generous | stingy |
| giving | taking |
| truthful | lying |
| punctual | late |
| helpful | hindrance |
| polite | rude |
| diligent | lazy |

7

| | |
|---|---|
| motivated | disinterested |
| happy | depressed |
| humorous | overserious |
| trustworthy | shifty |
| gentle | rough |
| content | anxious |
| peaceful | violent |
| sharing | selfish |
| enjoys physical contact | dislikes physical contact |
| enthusiastic | stick-in-the-mud |
| obedient | disobedient |
| creative | uncreative |
| imaginative | unimaginative |
| constructive | destructive |
| quick | slow |
| tenacious | stubborn |
| organized | disorganized |
| contributory | parasite |
| loving | hateful |
| law abiding | criminal |

Of course, these types of behaviors always occur as *specific acts* in a particular situation, and it is these acts which we modify with our programs.

Biting one's nails is a negative behavior. So are bullying other children, stealing, and getting dressed very slowly. Some examples of positive behaviors would be playing with other children cooperatively, coming when called once, and saying "please" when asking for something. Can you (the reader) discriminate between and isolate two separate behaviors when one child says to another, "Please shut your stupid mouth!" Saying "please" is a positive behavior—that of being polite, whereas "Shut your stupid mouth" is negative behavior as it degrades the person being spoken to. Think now of the more appropriate response to the chlidren.

*Goals and Objectives*

It is pertinent that we should be clear as to what our goals and objectives are for the child. This brings up ethical considerations which require the intervener to examine his or her own motives for wishing a specific behavior change to take place. One teacher will wish to extinguish a behavior as disruptive, while the same behavior is regarded by another teacher as a learning of social skills. Just the other day, two boys were fighting in the playground. One of the women teachers commented that the fight should be stopped as the children were learning to behave aggressively. However, a second teacher, a male, prevented any intervention because he felt that the boys were learning "to fight their own battles" and "to face life as it really is." Always be sure your goals for the child are (a) ethically defensible, (b) in the child's interests, and (c) not soley for one's own convenience.

### Behavior Setting

The behavior setting at any given moment refers to the surrounding environment and events which influence the particular behaviors emitted by the child at that time. Note that the "influence" may be passive or active. For the child or adult who gets a satisfaction (reward) from stealing, the self-service store is a *static behavior setting* which is highly likely to trigger off stealing behavior. An example of an *active behavior setting* would be a group of children playing a dice game together in which one of them cheats, and *then* a second child has a temper tantrum as a violent reaction to the cheating.

### Behavior Modification, Reinforcement Therapy, Behavior Therapy

These three terms all mean much the same—that is, the changing of behavior or the developing (building) of behavior quite deliberately by an intervener who sets up or organizes a reinforcement schedule for the purpose.

### Measurement of Behavior

The intervener must not only *discriminate* and *isolate* the behavior in question from other behaviors, he must also *measure* the extent and frequency of the specific behavior before starting any modification procedures. Measurement involves finding a *baseline* first.

### Baseline

The measurement of an existing behavior is called "obtaining a baseline." The best way to obtain a baseline is to observe (unnoticed) the child for several separate fixed periods of time, say any ten-minute period on each separate day for five days. During each ten minutes (or half hour or even an hour if the behavior is infrequent), count the number of times the particular behavior occurs. If a child is biting his nails, it may occur on the average of three times in every ten minutes over the five days of observations. Any behavior modification subsequent to this establishment of the baseline (three times every ten minutes) will hope to *decrease* the frequency of nail biting. This is done by observing (unnoticed if possible) the child once daily for a ten-minute interval throughout the training program. At the end of the training program, one can obtain a final observational frequency measurement which can then be compared statistically with the original baseline data. (This topic will be discussed in more detail with charts in Chapter V.)

The above example of biting nails concerned a *negative* behavior which was to be *decreased in frequency*. More often, as good teachers and parents, we will want to establish a baseline for a specific good (positive) behavior such as sharing toys or saying "please." Once again, to obtain a baseline, we observe the frequency of toy sharing for set intervals of time (ten minutes) once or twice during the day when play is occurring. Our behavior modification objective is now to *increase* the observed frequency of toy sharing which is a *positive* behavior. Exactly *how* this is done will be described later.

### Target Behavior

This is that specific isolated behavior which we wish to build, shape, modify, or extinguish. Note that the term "target response" is used to indicate the nature of the *desirable* behavior (even if it is *not* doing something) we wish the child to develop as a result of our program. We must *discriminate* this target behavior from others in the behavior setting. For example, our target behavior might be *abusive language* directed toward others. The target response would be *not being abusive* and we would have to discriminate abusive comments from genuine, helpful criticism.

### Motivation

To the behavioral psychologist, the term "motivation" is used in a very practical way; briefly, we learn to do things and want to do things because some rewarding satisfaction of one kind or another will follow our learning. We learn to cook delicious dishes for the reward of eating fine food. We learn to drive a car for a variety of social and timesaving reasons. But these are long-term, highly sophisticated, adult rewards and as such are meaningless to most children. Both children and adults are much more strongly motivated by the immediate reward or payoff (see below).

### Reinforcement

Although it is an oversimplification of the theory, we can say for the moment that reinforcement is a system of rewards and punishment which follows as soon as possible after the specific behavior we wish to modify has occurred. In short, we reward specific "good" or positive behaviors immediately and do not reward unacceptable ones. Of course, the definition of reinforcement calls for much more elaboration and precision and further details are set out below.

For example, if Bobby enjoys being hugged and we immediately give him a big hug each time he cleans his teeth, then the positive behavior of teeth cleaning will become established. If Matthew repeatedly draws lines on the walls and we make him scrub them off immediately (holding his hand if necessary), he will cease drawing on the walls. Note that these examples are deliberately oversimplified and that they are based on the assumption that the child is receiving a "normal" amount of real adult affection at appropriate times during the day. *It is much more difficult to modify positive or negative behaviors in a child who is unloved or who feels himself to be unloved.* This problem will be dealt with more fully in Chapter VI (see "The Importance of Parent and Child Enjoying Each Other").

### Response, Response Behavior

The response or response behavior is that target behavior which we wish the child to possess. The word response comes from traditonal or classical conditioning theory, such as occurs in the Seaquarium when the bell is rung (stimulus cue) and the fish respond by coming to eat (response). The response, then, is that behavioral activity which we wish the child or any other organism to learn. In our previous examples, the responses would be (a) cleaning teeth (b) not drawing on the walls. Not infrequently, it is not so much the *act* which is to be learned (*e.g.* eating) as the *time* (to eat) or the *signal* (to eat).

## Stimulus, Stimuli

The stimulus (or in the plural form, stimuli) is any environmental event or structured situation designed to bring forth a required response from an individual. Put simply, one stimulates another person to bring forth a specific response. A common adult example might be a sexual response to a passionate kiss. All too often, the stimulus is not sufficiently clear to the child, as for example, when he is to clean his teeth or go to bed. Parents may be annoyed with their child because he did not clean his teeth or go to bed even though there was no regular clear-cut stimulus signal to do so. A kitchen timer or twenty-four-hour alarm set by the mother can often eliminate such vague stimuli and substitute a regular signalled routine. Note that there are an infinite number of stimuli inside and outside us and that they may occur *before or after* our response.

## Operant Response

This type of response occurs *before* the stimulus occurs, because past memories of similar or preferably identical situations remind us that if we do such and such (the response) a certain desirable stimulus will be forthcoming. For example, we learn that if we put a quarter into the vending machine (the *operant response*), we will be rewarded with the "stimulus" of candy or a soda drink (also called the reinforcer). A little later in this book we will drop the word *stimulus* althogether because its uses by psychologists are many and confusing.

## Operant Conditioning

Operant conditioning occurs when a person (the operator or subject) operates on his environment (which may include his own body) to bring about an event or change in the total situation. An *operant* then is any response behavior which produces or changes some subsequent (stimulus) event. In the example above, the operant behavior or response is the inserting of the quarter in the machine and the (stimulus) event or effected change is receiving and drinking the soda or eating the candy. Once a child has learned that inserting a quarter in the machine produces candy or soda, and he can do the task efficiently, he is said to be operantly conditioned to perform that particular task.

## Reinforcer, Reinforcing Stimulus

The (positive) reinforcing stimulus or *reinforcer* is that particular event or change in circumstances which rewards the individual in a *satisfying* way. In the above example, the receiving and eating of candy is a reinforcer or reinforcing stimulus. *Reinforcers* are all-important in behavior modification as they are the reward the child or adult receives for performing the operant act or behavior which we as parents want. Positive reinforcers are almost invariably satisfying in some way; that is, they fulfill some need the person has. There are many kinds of reinforcers, such as drinks, food, praise, money, tokens or points, hugs and kisses, smiles, outings, television, toys, equipment, treats. Of course, most of these do not always reinforce. Only when they are awarded after some act or behavior as a reward do they technically become reinforcers. If you give your son a watch at graduation, it is a reinforcer; if you give him one for his birthday as a present, it is *not* a reinforcer— it does not follow as a *contingent consequence* to some act or behavior.

Note that not all reinforcers are positive in their effect on people. If society wishes to prevent speeding drivers, it does not reward them with money when they are caught. Instead, the driver is fined (a very unsatisfying experience). This is a good example of a negative reinforcer. In the home and school, spankings, sarcasm, abusive language, deprivation of privileges such as TV, and time out in one's bedroom are all examples of the everyday negative reinforcer's used with children.

The above introduction to the concepts of positive and negative reinforcement will be elaborated in much greater detail in later sections and chapters.

## Trial and Error Behavior

When a child or adult is initially learning a particular operant behavior which will produce a *satisfying* reinforcing stimulus (reinforcer), he may, in certain situations, make several or many erroneous trials (perhaps mixed with successful ones) before he achieves success almost every time. Trial and error behavior is most frequently seen in unstructured situations in which the child receives no help. For example, many children learn to ride a two-wheeled bicycle without instruction, and they usually fall off many times before they "get the hang of it." Incidentally, the reinforcing stimulus in this case is the satisfaction of being able to ride like other children, and to be able to transport oneself quickly from one place to another. Unfortunately, many schoolchildren learn and mislearn much of the work presented to them in the classroom in a trial and error way. Consequently, many children go through life without understanding many of the facts and principles they have failed to learn. It should be noted that trial and error behavior is a most inefficient form of learning because it teaches failure and will dismay most children, leaving them with a poor self-concept (opinion of their own abilities). Ideally, every child should experience regular success by learning through the easy steps of a well-programmed activity curriculum. Later, we will further investigate why many children do not learn effectively in school.

### Intervention, Intervener

When someone such as a teacher, parent, or psychologist deliberately plans to modify the behavior of an individual, it is said to be an *intervention* in the behavioral life of that individual. Intervention techniques, then, are carefully planned programs designed to modify behavior quite deliberately. The person who intervenes in the behavior of another in order to modify it is called an *intervener*. *Operant conditioning is an intervention technique,* or to be more accurate, a variety of intervention techniques. Planned operant conditioning intervention is a much more effective technique than leaving a child to learn his repertoire of behaviors on a trial and error basis. There are several categories of programmed intervention which we will now summarize.

### Modifying Behavior

This is a blanket term which covers *any kind of intervention aimed at altering the present behavior* or even lack of behavior in an individual. The words "modifying" or "modification" should be used only in a broad generic sense; it is better to use a more specific word when you are planning a particular type of intervention in the behavioral life of a person. The following definitions give examples of these specific terms in use.

## *Shape, Shaping Behavior*

Strictly speaking, the intervener *shapes* the behavior of the child or subject when a behavior already exists which needs altering in some way. For example, a child may already have a verbal response such as "Gimme a cookie," which we wish to shape or reshape. The reshaped verbal behavior which we wish to establish in the child might be, "May I please have a cookie, Mommy." This alteration of the verbal behavior which already exists is most easily achieved by telling a child what the correct words are (the operant response) and by giving him a cookie (the operant reinforcer) only when he uses the desired words. If, when the child uses the correct words, the mother says "No, you cannot have the cookie because it is five minutes before dinnertime," the whole shaping program will break down.

## *Building or Instating New Behavior*

What if there is no existing behavior to reshape? Very often, the intervener (parent, teacher, or psychologist) is in the position of desiring to *establish* a specific behavior (operant response) in a child or adult where one does not exist. In such a situation, the new behavior must be built or instated. To build behavior, we set up an operant conditioning program within a planned behavior setting which optimizes the likelihood of the desired operant response occurring. For example, if we wish a child to learn the social skills of how to greet people, we must place him in social behavior settings which allow him to meet people. Alternately, we can *role play* (see Ch. VI) behavior settings in which people are greeted. In such a behavior setting, the usual operant stimulus reinforcer is joyous praise following the child's successful operant response. Examples of behavior we may wish to build in children are politeness, friendliness, cheerfulness, and enjoyment of work. Politeness can be built by quickly giving the child what he requests whenever he says please. Also, if he does not say please, he must then wait a full minute before he asks a second time using the word *please*. He is then given the thing he requested. If he does not say thank you, the object he requested is taken back for one minute and the whole procedure is reenacted with both "please" and "thank you" included. Praise the child whenever he *does* say thank you or please.

The other behaviors mentioned can be built with both praise and privilege reinforcers. For example, say "You are a very friendly (or cheerful) boy this morning. What a wonderful thing you are making."

## Reducing or Extinguishing Behaviors

We may wish to *reduce* the frequency with which some behaviors occur because they take up too much of the child's time and may disturb others. An example of a behavior in the classroom which the teacher may wish to reduce would be that of a child who talks too much all the time. Naturally, the teacher would not wish to eliminate the child's talking altogether. Therefore, she would set up a program aimed at *reducing* the frequency of the child's verbal behavior (the operant response). This *reduction* in verbal behavior without entirely eliminating it in a child might be achieved with a program which offered the child in question a point for every ten minutes during which she spoke not more than once. The points (the operant stimulus reinforcer) might be cashed in later in the day or week for a toy, a certificate, or a pleasant letter from the teacher to the parents. *Extinguished behavior* is the term used when the operant response is to be *eliminated* completely. There are many examples of behaviors which parents and teachers unanimously like to extinguish: spitting, swearing, lying, running away, being cheeky, cruelty, damaging or destroying property, or persecuting other children are a few examples. The complete extinction of socially undesirable behaviors is best achieved through a *combination* of the operant techniques of negative and positive reinforcement (see Ch. III). Extinction is most rapid when an *acceptable alternative* behavior is introduced into the environment and is positively reinforced. For example, if we reinforce truthfulness with rewards, then lying should decrease.

## Elicit

This term has been used several times already and we are now in a position to define it. The words *elicit* or *elicitation* should only be used as an attribute of the child or person being conditioned (the respondent). As interveners, we may speak of desiring to elicit a certain type of behavior in or from the child (the respondent). Strictly speaking, it is the individual who elicits the desired behavior in himself in response to a stimulus. It is psychologically incorrect to say that the reinforcement elicits a response behavior.

*Strengthen*

Any response behavior (such as politeness) may be strengthened in three ways.

1. The frequency with which the "correct" behavior occurs may increase, provided the reinforcer is always available. The word *frequency* in this case is used in a special sense. Usually, when we wish to shape a specific behavior we wish the child to respond correctly everytime the stimulus is presented. For example, we may wish a child to say thank you everytime he is given something. Thus, the success rate (frequency) should ideally reach 100 percent, and we wish to strengthen behavior to this level. However, the frequency of success (the strength) may only be 60 percent of the possible upper limit. In this case, the child would be saying thank you only six times out of every ten.

2. The second way in which strength is used in operant conditioning is in the sense of the magnitude of one individual response. Of course, this applies only to those kinds of responses which allow for magnitude such as noise, verbal behavior, physical strength, food consumption, speed, and emotional reactions generally. An example of this type of *magnitude strength* would be the distance a child can swim in terms of lengths of the pool—is it 10, 20, 50, 100, or 500 yards.

3. Strength may also be measured in a third way, namely, the *length of time* it takes for a person to respond once they have been stimulated to respond (see next definition).

*The Initial Cue or Discriminant Stimulus*

In any behavior setting, there always has to be a stimulus or *initial cue* which sets the whole train of behavior from operant response to reinforcement stimulus in motion. These events are triggered by the initial cue or discriminant stimulus. For example, when a child is given a quarter, he runs for the vending machine in order to get his candy or soda. In this case, the quarter itself is an initial cue or discriminant stimulus or signal that, if he performs a certain operation with that quarter (puts it in the slot of the vending machine) then certain pleasurable consequences will follow as a reinforcement (he gets the candy or drink). *Note that the word "stimulus" has now been used in two ways; in order to avoid ambiguity, we will henceforth use only the word "cue" or "initial cue" to mean the discriminant stimulus.* The word "discriminant" has been used here because the subject must *discriminate* what the cue or initial stimulus is before he can operate it. For example, the child must know that the quarter can be used in a vending machine before he can operate the machine. Therefore, he has to discriminate a quarter from a dime, a nickel, and a penny in order to use it successfully. We can now see that the operant conditioning situation consists of (a) a *discriminant initial cue* followed by (b) an *operant response* on the part of the individual who is (c) *reinforced* by a reinforcer or *operant stimulus* (the reinforcing candy or drink). The word "discriminant" can describe responses as well as cues (see below).

## Discriminant Response or Operant Response

Just as the child had to discriminate (learn) that a quarter was different from a dime, so too must he learn to distinguish between the candy vending machine, the cigarette vending machine, and the soda vending machine. Furthermore, he must distinguish (discriminate) between the slot where the quarters go in, the slot where change is returned, and other parts of the machine. Therefore, quite a lot of *discriminant learning* takes place in the operant phase of the conditioning procedure. In most learning situations, the intervener's *objective* is frequently to establish a single isolated chain of behavioral actions and events which are uncontaminated by other events. An example would be when mother says to her son, "It is time for dinner" (initial cue), and the son goes to the bathroom, washes his hands (a discriminant operant response), and returns to the table to eat (a reinforcing stimulus). The discriminative (operant) response may have reached its sharpened, well-learned state only after many learning trials. For example, Robin went to the bathroom to wash his hands but instead he played with the soap for fifteen minutes thoroughly decorating the mirror with soapy handprints in the process. He had not learned to discriminate the play response from the task response of washing his hands quickly. This discrimination of play from hand washing was explained verbally and the negative reinforcer was to miss the first course of the meal—his favorite sphaghetti. The process of sorting out (by the child or subject) *which* specific response is to be discriminated from all the possible ones is called *response differentiation* (next definition).

## Response Differentiation

In the earlier example above, response differentiation occurred when the child learned in which *machine* to put the quarter in order to receive candy. He differentiated one action out of three others that were possible. A better example of *response differentiation* is the case of a young child learning to manipulate correctly the control knobs on a television set. If he does not select the correct knob and move it in the right way, he is not reinforced with a reasonable picture (the reinforcing stimulus). Therefore, over a period of time and using a trial and error technique (if he is not instructed) selecting and moving the *wrong* controls will be gradually extinguished, while the selection and movement of the *correct* controls will be finally differentiated as a correct response which is reinforced successfully with a clear picture on the screen. Note that the term "discriminative response" is synonymous with the term "differentiated response"; both mean the specific response which the intervener (and usually the subject) wishes the subject to learn.

## Initial Cue Generalization

For example, Lynne had been successfully conditioned to feed herself with a spoon at mealtime. One day her mother put a knife down near her plate and the infant, seeing the knife, promptly shoved it in her mouth. Her action with the knife had been *generalized* from what she does with a spoon when she sees one. Fork, knife, and spoon all go into her mouth in much the same way and the *positioning of them* all on the table by her mother where they can be seen and grasped by Lynne is an initial cue generalization (also called a "stimulus generalization," though this latter term is very confusing as the words in it are used ambiguously).

## Response Generalization

Response generalization is the opposite to response differentiation. When a child has been consistently reinforced for a particular response behavior or group of response behaviors, he is quite likely to extend these responses to include other *similar responses* in the hope that these will be reinforced in the same way. For example, if Frank has received fifty cents for mowing the lawn, he may promptly ask if he can trim the hedge for another fifty cents. Bruce was praised for learning one type of dive into the swimming pool and promptly generalized it to other types of dives and swimming feats. Kate is a seven-year-old girl who will always paint six pictures in a row because she is invariably praised after completing each one.

## The Reinforcer as a Cue

To avoid ambiguity, let us now *drop the word "stimulus" altogether* and use the following terms to denote the three stages of an operant conditioning situation; (a) the initial cue or more briefly, cue, (b) the operant response or response, and (c) the reinforcer or reinforcement.

In our example of the candy vending machine, the sight of the *candy* through the glass window of the machine is often itself an initial cue for pushing the quarter into the machine in order to get the *candy* as a reinforcer. In other words, as *objects,* the initial cue and the reinforcer are sometimes identical.

## Acquired Reinforcers

Let us assume that our boy Frank, who mowed the lawn and cut the hedge, likes candy and that he has already *learned* that quarters operate the candy vending machine. The candy reinforces Frank to work the machine, but to work the machine he must have money; to get the money, Frank must mow the lawn—the money reinforces him to mow the lawn. In the one instance, the money is a reinforcer and in the other it is the cue; for this boy, the money is technically called an acquired reinforcer—the money has the equivalence and value of candy because it can buy candy. Money is an acquired reinforcer for the entire human race because the things it buys are often reinforcers. They satisfy or fulfill basic human survival needs. However, any reinforcer which was once (and still remains) an initial cue leading to a powerful basic reinforcer (food, drink, rest, sex, pleasure, and so on) and which has been learned as such, is called an acquired reinforcer. Other examples of acquired reinforcers of this kind are trading stamps, coupons, credit cards, free gifts in cereal packages, and the like. (See Chapter III for more about acquired reinforcers.)

## Verbal Behavior

As mentioned previously, verbal behavior consists of talking, whispering, screaming, shouting, grunting—in fact, making any kind of communicative noise. Strictly speaking, the term used should be "verbal and vocal behavior," but it is generally understood that verbal behavior stands for both. However, when discussing particular programs it is always best to state the particular *type* of verbal behavior in question, for example, shouting or whining. Many verbal behaviors can be modified by operant conditioning. Sam is a good example. Whenever he spoke to his mother, he would whine and she in turn would berate him for it in an impatient voice that, in its own way, was as negative and habitual as Sam's whining. To modify Sam's verbal behavior, his mother adopted a completely new policy. Each time he whined he was *pleasantly* told he would have to wait one minute to receive whatever it was he had requested (the reinforcer) and then only if he asked again in his *"own happy voice"* at the end of that minute. Mother never referred to Sam's whining directly; she always stressed his happy voice (her own was now happy too) so that he became identified with it as his *own* normal voice. Whenever he spontaneously used his "own happy voice," and he soon did so frequently, she praised him for it and granted his request immediately.

## Rate of Acquisition of Behavior

It is possible to plot on a graph or to tabulate the number of times each day (or ten minutes or hour) that the new behavior which we hope to build, shape, or modify in some way occurs in the subject. The resulting curve or increase day by day indicates the rate at which the new behavior is being acquired and this is called the rate of acquisition. Usually, the rate of acquisition takes off slowly, so to speak, then rises steeply until it levels off in a high percentage success rate which means that the new behavior has become established. Sam's happy voice may have occurred on average only once or twice a day the first week, three times a day the second week, and twelve times a day the third week.

## To Accelerate or Decelerate Behavior

This is just a way of commenting on the *rate* of the acquisition of a new behavior. It is convenient to speak of accelerating or decelerating the occurrence of a particular behavior through the use of operant techniques. Sam's rate of acquisition of a happy voice was an accelerating one (2, 3, 12, 30, etc.) while conversely, his rate of whinig was a decelerating one. Note that when we are reducing a behavior or extinguishing it, the terms "rate of extinction" and "deceleration" are the appropriate ones to use.

*Chapter III*

# POSITIVE REINFORCEMENT

T HERE ARE SEVERAL TYPES of reinforcement which can be used
to modify, shape, build, reduce, or extinguish behavior, and the
most important one of all is *positive reinforcement*. At its very
simplest, positive reinforcement is the giving of a "reward" to the
subject immediately after the operant response which we desire
him to perform has been completed. The implications of positive
reinforcement in the life of the child are many and call for some
discussion.

If most of us examine both our own childhoods and our lives
today, we much prefer to live with and work for people who are
kind, pleasant, encouraging, who pay us well, who praise us frequently, and who recognize and appreciate our efforts to do a good
job. On the other hand, we dislike living with or working for people
who are constantly nagging, who belittle and depreciate our efforts,
who antagonize us with constant criticism, who are abusive, who
pick up every little error, who are dictatorial, who chastise us,
and who constantly tell us we are a little no-good or its equivalent.
Yet almost all of us as parents and teachers continue to operate
much more on the negative system just mentioned than on the
positive reinforcement system. Research has shown that there are
very few parents or teachers who, when in contact with children,
use positive statements more frequently than they use negative
statements. In a later section, we will discuss the ideal proportions
of positive to negative reinforcement when working with children.

Many parents and particularly teachers feel strongly (and we
would emphasize the subjective word *feel*) that children should
work for their parents and teachers out of love and duty and a
spontaneous joy of life. In practical terms, this is as unrealistic

23

as saying that right now *everybody* in every community should no longer commit any crimes, tell any lies, or be angry, and should always be selfless in every action involving others. The day that love and duty take over the earth, *even for adults* (let alone children), is a very long way off and yet these teachers and parents are expecting little children to have moral and ethical standards of behavior which only one adult in a million sometimes achieves. Frankly, it is very unrealistic, although of course the idealistic motives are extremely worthy. What, then, do we do in the meantime while waiting for the human race to evolve to this heaven on earth? As always, we have to take the next realistic step from the situation as it is. That next step is positive reinforcement and we must use every specific reinforcer we know of, can discover, or can invent to help our children along the road toward a responsible, enriching personal and social life. Many children are not yet even at the stage of being able to accept praise or encouragement as a reinforcer for the tasks they perform in school or at home. This is unfortunate, but in the largely negative environment of the school and home, these children have not been conditioned to accept these positive social reinforcers. Therefore, it may be necessary to use more primary rewards (reinforcers) such as free time, having the privilege of using equipment, acquiring objects (stamps, pictures, etc.) for their personal collection, or even such everyday things as candy, soda, pretzels, pickles, cereal, raisins, or a myriad of other enjoyable foods.

Some teachers and parents, particularly those who wish to bring about love and duty in their children, suggest that material reinforcers of the type just described are bribery and that the children thus acquire a commercial set of values which, presumably, will be to their detriment in later life. This is a double misunderstanding— a misunderstanding of the meaning of the word bribery and a misunderstanding of how social values are learned. First of all, bribery is only applicable to illegal situations. Some people bribe a policeman not to give them a ticket, while others may bribe a judge, administrator, or political personage for special favors. Additionally, in bribery the "reward" comes *before* the response, not contingently after it. The policeman is handed the money and then he does not write out the ticket. This is *not* what happens in operant conditioning. Reinforcement for the child must always come after the act and be contingent on it.

In enlightened families, some children have learned almost from birth to respond to strong, positive, social reinforcement in the form of smiles, praise, encouragement, laughter, tickling, romping, caressing, cuddling, hair rumpling, doing things together, and so on. For such fortunate children, these excellent social reinforcers largely eliminate any need-dependence on primary reinforcers such as foods and other materials which give pleasure. Most children, however, have to have their responses to social reinforcers *built* into them, or have the weak responses they already possess strengthened to the point where they can be useful for operant conditioning purposes.

On the other hand, it is the adults in the environment who have the *responsibility and duty* to set about acquiring and using positive social reinforcers as characteristics of their own personalities when managing children. The mother, father, teacher, nurse, and care worker must *learn* how to praise, encourage, hug, caress, grin, laugh, and give pleasure quite spontaneously to children whenever they complete a task in *any* situation.

Little Stephanie was praised, hugged, and gurgled over by her mother, father, and older brothers until she was two years old. When she first walked, everyone clapped including Stephanie. Her first words were greeted with cries of delight and Stephanie enjoyed not only repeating them on demand but also adding new words daily. When she was one and a half years of age, a subtle change occurred in Stephanie's world. Her "innocent" negative behavior such as tearing books, breaking toys, throwing tantrums when frustrated, turning off the television, spilling food, and screaming was soon counteracted by the entire family (once the novelty wore off and it was no longer baby-cute) with shouts ("Stop it!"), shoves ("Get away from there!"), spanks ("Don't shout like that!"), and nagging ("I've told you a hundred times that's a no-no!"). Nearly all the considerable love and affection that Stephanie gets is now reserved for nonlearning situations ("Cuddle up and I'll read you a story," "Everyone kiss Stephanie goodnight," "Let's play the tickling game"). Praise and encouragement for learning situations is almost forgotten because learning *positively* is also a thing of the past. Stephanie's life has become one of having *limits* set in a very negative way. Most important of all, *Stephanie is not taught positive ways to solve her frustrating problems,* so she battles on, imitating her mother, father, and brothers, learning to shout, shove, spank, and nag. How can Stephanie be taught positive ways to solve her problems? It is really simple. (1) *Find out* what it is she wants to do (tear up books). (2) *Devise* a new way of letting her achieve this new skill (tearing up sheaves of paper). (3) *Provide* the necessary equipment and materials (old magazines). (4) *Teach* her to *discriminate* between the operant responses (tearing up valuable books and tearing *her* old magazines). (5) *Positively reinforce* her for the correct response (tearing up old magazines). Use praise, delight, encouraging demonstrations, and so forth, as positive reinforcement. (6) Negatively reinforce her for the incorrect response of *reaching for* the valuable books. Put them out of reach. For negative reinforcement, use a strong No-No combined with a *gentle* placing of Stephanie by the old magazines. Note that the positive reinforcement should occur much more frequently than the negative. More will be said about positive training and problem solving in Chapter VI.

In the context of the above comments, we can now proceed with further definitions and explanations.

## Positive Reinforcers

Positive reinforcers are any objects or reactions in people or pleasant situations which the child or subject has a need for, wishes to possess, or wants to achieve. Positive reinforcers always involve *approach behavior* in the sense that the child will approach toward (psychologically speaking) the reinforcer in order to get it. In the case of social reinforcers, the child will approach the intervener. Some authorities have defined positive reinforcers as those which increase behavior, but it is possible to positively reward a child for decreasing and eliminating certain types of behavior. Robert was rewarded for *not* hitting children, or screaming, or having tantrums at school by having his mother lie on the bed with him for ten minutes while he was going to sleep at the end of each day in which these negative behaviors had *not* occurred. To call this positive action on the part of the mother a negative reinforcer because the child's screaming and hitting episodes were *decreasing* is just too semantically confusing. Therefore, in this book positive reinforcement describes the reinforcement itself and is not dependent on whether behavior is built, eliminated, strengthened, or weakened.

## Reward

This term has a much broader popular meaning than reinforcer and should only be used in a context which defines its limitations. If one *contracts* (see below) with children, as for example would be the case when you say to your child "Please mow the lawn and I will give you two dollars," then strictly speaking the two dollars is a reward, not a reinforcer. In fact, it is payment like any salary. To call such contracting "bribery" (see above) is as erroneous as saying that your salary when you work for an organization is not a salary but a bribe to work.

## Payoff

This too is a wider term than reinforcer. In fact, it is usually used to connote the circumstantial reinforcer which rewards the child for bad behavior. If Harry steals from another boy, the payoff is the loot he gets and perhaps the thrill, satisfaction, or emotional "kick" he receives when stealing. If Elizabeth "cons" her mother into giving her a cookie to be a good girl (note, she is operantly modifying her mother's behavior with the reinforcer of "good girl"), Elizabeth's payoff is the cookie. The adult should always try to discover the payoff for a child's undesirable behavior and eliminate it as a necessary *part* of the program of extinguishing that negative behavior.

## Circumstantial Reinforcer

This term refers to the rewards a child or adult receives in the everyday environment which maintains all kinds of behavior ranging from the socially acceptable to true antisocial behaviors. The word *circumstantial* is used to imply that the cue, response, and reinforcer as an overall recurring life situation have been learned or acquired spontaneously without any *deliberate* planning or awareness of what was happening on the part of the intervener or usually on the part of the subject. Thus, to repeat what was said above, when we analyze the antisocial behavior of children or adults it is wise (on the part of the intervener) to search out the payoffs or circumstantial reinforcers which maintain the undesirable behavior. The reason is simple—if we eliminate the circumstantial reinforcer (payoff) we are well on the way to eliminating the negative behavior being reinforced. Note that circumstantial reinforcers can also be positive, e.g. the pleasure from reading novels is a direct result of having learned to read.

## Contingent, Contingency

These words have been used several times already, but they require very precise definition. In operant theory, *contingent* means that one event (usually the reinforcer) occurs immediately or soon after another event (usually the operant response). Numerous researches have shown that operant conditioning is quicker, longer lasting, and more effective in every way the *sooner* the reinforcer occurs after the operant response is made. If Ben solves a new mathematical problem correctly in the middle of a lesson, it is much better to praise him and give him an achievement credit right there and then than to wait until the end of the lesson or worse still, the end of the week to do so. Reinforcers are heavily dependent on *memory*, particularly the memory associating the response task (solving the problem) with the credit it deserves (the praise or mark given). It cannot be stressed too strongly that a child or adult must be *immediately rewarded* (reinforced) contingently upon the successful completion of the response task.

Sometimes, the situation or circumstances prevents the reinforcer from being immediately contingent upon the response. For example, a parent is unable to spend all day in the classroom to prevent a child from hitting others or screaming, and the teacher may not understand or be interested in operant conditioning. Therefore, the parent has no alternative but to wait until the end of the day to reinforce her child. In the case of the mother lying with the child while he went to sleep, a more immediate reinforcer was possible—on collecting the child from school, the mother praised her son when she ascertained from the teacher that he had not hit anyone or screamed in school that day. Along with her praise, she mentioned to the son that she would stay with him for ten minutes when he went to sleep that night.

When reinforcing a behavior with an immediately contingent "reward," make sure that no other behavior gets in between the one you wish to reinforce and the reinforcer itself. This can sabotage the whole operation. Mrs. Shell, after attending a behavior modification course, decided to reinforce her son Len for allowing her to brush his hair each morning. This operation had always resulted in sceams, protests, and tears (mother's impatience with his behavior had always made her brush very briskly). So Mrs. Shell began giving Len a piece of sugarless chewing gum after gently brushing his hair; unfortunately, however, she always went to the kitchen to find the gum, by which time Len was in the middle of a real tantrum. Mrs. Shell wondered why the screams increased; she did not realize she was reinforcing the tantrums—*not* the pleasant hair-brushing operation. Ideally, Mrs. Shell would have (a) carried the unwrapped gum in her pocket, (b) reduced her total hair-brushing for the first day to two light strokes, (c) given him the gum immediately after the total hair-brushing operation of two strokes, (d) ensured that the gum was given after the two strokes but before he could cry or even wanted to cry, (e) increased the brushing operation *one* extra light stroke a day, always immediately giving him the gum.

## Intermediate Reinforcers

Note that it is also legitimate to reinforce a child's behavior *during* the behavior, especially if that behavior calls for the *additional* behavior of sustained effort. This occurs spontaneously when the athletics coach shouts "You're ahead of time" *each* time the runner circles the track in a mile run of four laps. The teacher who, while watching Mary solve a long division problem step by step, says to her once or twice, "You *are* a good worker, Mary," is reinforcing her efforts and diligence. In both these instances, the final contingent reinforcer to be effective must be stronger than the intermediate ones.

## Multiple Reinforcers

In the example of the praise after school and the mother lying in bed with the child later in the evening, the two reinforcers together are termed "multiple reinforcers." Whenever the intervener uses two or more quite *separate* reinforcers for the same operant response, they are termed multiple reinforcers.

## Primary Reinforcers

These usually are food, drink, candy. They are called *primary* because they seem to occur naturally wtihout having to be deliberately endowed with reinforcement power through learning. Some psychologists suggest that primary reinforcers satisfy basic human drives such as hunger, thirst, and sex. Primary reinforcers include the reduction or the *removal* of fear or pain.

## Social Reinforcers

Another group of positive reinforcers are the social reinforcers. These are smiles, caresses, kisses, cuddles, praise, encouragement, and so on, which have also been previously described above. Some pychologists claim that these have to be entirely learned, but research over the last ten years suggests that affection (technically called "attachment" and some of its demonstrative behaviors may be predominantly in-built (innate) even though they may be somewhat modified by environmental events; but then, all primary reinforcers can also be modified by environmental events. Whatever their origins (innate or learned, or more likely both innate *and* learned), social reinforcers are much more convenient, economical, immediately contingent, and just as powerful as primary reinforcers. This does *not* mean social reinforcers are interchangeable with primary ones in any given situation.

## Acquired (Learned) Reinforcers

In addition to the items mentioned in Chapter II, television, painting, using a record player, collecting objects, driving cars, going to a movie, and so forth, are all *learned or acquired positive reinforcers* which most people find enjoyable. When used contingently as reinforcers following a desired response, they are called "acquired reinforcers" (*not* primary).

## Token Reinforcers

In place of primary reinforcers, it is often more convenient and economical to give the child  points or tokens which me may *later* cash in for primary reinforcers or sometimes social reinforcers (e.g. certificates). These tokens, which may be plastic, metal, or points on a chart or in a notebook, have many obvious advantages for the schoolteacher. Indeed, in the history of education, they have been used for at least a century. Token economies have been used extensively in schools and institutions with considerable success; they provide the teacher with a continuous, powerful, management control system which has many advantages over unorganized, sporadic reinforcement by the teacher. It is worth noting again that money is a form of token reinforcer for the whole human race.

## Non-Reinforcers

The distinction between a reinforcer and a nonreinforcer needs to be made clear. Any object, service, token, symbol, or social contact (including interpersonal ones) is *only* a reinforcer if and when it is contingent in some systematic way with one particular behavior. Otherwise, it is a nonoperant event in one's life which has little or no bearing on operant learning. Therefore, kissing can be a "nonoperant event," or it can be a powerful reinforcer when it follows one specific behavior, as for example a child coming home on time. Money can be a gift (an allowance) or a reinforcer for a good job of work. The latter case is the preferred one.

Note that nonreinforcers are very valid experiences in their own right. It would be a sad world if we only kissed others as a reinforcer, or if we only gave food contingently on some learning situation.

## Neutral Stimulus

We have reverted to the use of the word "stimulus" this once because the term "neutral reinforcer" would be a verbal contradiction. A neutral stimulus is one which was neither a negative nor a positive reinforcement *value* for the subject as a contingent event after a very specific response. Thus, in keeping with the old adage that "One man's meat is another man's poison," a double Scotch might be a powerful reinforcer to one man but not to another.

## Converting a Neutral Stimulus into an Acquired Postive Reinforcer Through Pairing

By pairing a neutral stimulus with a positive reinforcer (usually primary) and making the pair contingent upon the operant response, we change the value of the neutral stimulus and turn it into an *acquired positive reinforcer.* This is a very useful technique for developing social reinforcers in those children who do not possess them. Many children respond only to primary reinforcers such as candy. If every time such a child is given candy the intervener says "Good boy!" the neutral stimulus (for this child) "Good boy!" will become indelibly associated with the primary reinforcer, the candy. Before long, if the program is effective, the pairing of the phrase "Good boy!" with the candy will result in the child being reinforced by the phrase "Good boy!" without the need for candy. Obviously, it is best to withdraw the candy *slowly* as the relationship between intervener and child develops. Only the naive would suggest that the phrase "Good boy!" as a verbal statement is the total acquired reinforcer. What is really happening is that the child is developing an affection for the intervener which becomes a need in itself. This need for affection (or for praise which is one form of affection) is partially associated each time the phrase "Good boy!" is used.

In a research done by one of the authors, *praise* and similar social/emotional reinforcers were found to be the most important part of an academic learning program for one child. (See Ch. VI for more about "praise.") Thus, it can be seen that over a period of time, acquired reinforcers of any kind can be built or established by *pairing them* with a powerful reinforcer which already exists.

## Summary of the Differences Between Primary, Acquired, and Social Reinforcers

Primary (positive) reinforcers are those which satisfy (or reduce if they cause discomfort) basic natural human physiological needs. The drives of hunger, thirst, sleep, sex, pain, and exercise are examples of primary drives. Examples of common primary reinforcers are candy, soft drinks, and cereal.

Acquired reinforcers are themselves learned—one acquires a "taste" for them. We *learn* to like television or money or trading stamps or toys.

Social reinforcers are a special category (in this book) which includes all interpersonal relationships and contacts either within a group or between two people. Some authorities classify social reinforcers as acquired, but others (including the authors) classify them as primary reinforcers inasmuch as attachment has been demonstrated to be a basic human drive in primates.

## Consistency of the Intervener

One of the most important aspects of any operant conditioning program is that the intervener must insure that the same sequence of operant events (cue, response, and reinforcement) occurs in an identical way each time the behavior setting occurs or is set up by the intervener. One of the most common causes of an operant program failing is the *lack of consistency* in giving the reinforcer contingently on the desired response. It is worth repeating again for emphasis that *consistency by the intervener* is an operant conditioning program is of paramount importance to its success. Mrs. Reynolds sought the advice of a psychologist because her son Bill refused to come home on time after school. She did not find that physical punishment decreased the negative behavior—in fact, if anything, more spanking made him stay out even longer. Bill was put on a points reinforcement program; each time he came home from school directly and on time he was to be awarded five points. For every ten minutes he was late, he would receive one point less. At the end of each week on Saturday, he would be taken to the department store to purchase a toy to the value of his points (possible top value $1.50). Bill was also to be loudly praised in front of the family every time he came home on time. The system worked very well for six weeks until Mrs. Reynolds (a) missed two Saturday morning visits to the store, (b) began shouting angrily at Bill when he was late, and (c) could not be bothered calculating his points accurately. Bill was bright and resented these inconsistencies and took to staying out again because it was all "unfair" and "Mom did not keep her promise." After counseling, Mrs. Reynolds began to see how she was not following through and that she was defeating her own ends by being so inconsistent. After another six months, Bill was always coming home on time and he would first ask permission if he wished to go out. His reinforcement points program was extended to cover other facets of his behavior and a set of contracts to do odd jobs around the house was implemented. The praising and affection were increased in amount and widened in application to form a solid multiple reinforcement system with the points.

## Structured Learning Situations (Programs)

Very frequently, it is possible to construct a structured learning situation so that the sequence of events (cue, response, reinforcer) and even the initiation of the sequence (by cue) is entirely under the control of the intervener. This is most easily done in the home or in the classroom, but once again consistency is most important. For example, if we wish to reinforce children in the classroom for working quietly, being interested, staying in their seats, being cooperative, and talking only in quiet voices, we can set a timer to ring every twenty minutes and give all the children a point on prepared cards for each of these good behaviors if they have been successful in each of them. For convenience, the children would checkmark their own cards. Thus, a teacher is able to positively reinforce specific acceptable behaviors in a deliberately structured situation completely under his own control.* In the home, a child could be given a dozen peanuts or raisins, which would be put on his plate every time he came to a meal the *first* time he was called. The cue would be the mother's call, the operant response would be the child's coming to table, and the reinforcer would be the peanuts or raisins or any other small piece of nutritious, savory food. Favorite television programs can become excellent reinforcers for homework sessions, especially if praise and encouragement is also given while the homework is being done.

*A comprehensive classroom program of behavior management and motivation compiled by the authors and entitled, *Motivation Management Materials,* is published by the Kismet Publishing Co., P.O. Box 90, South Miami, Fla. 33156.

## Physical Structuring and Prompts

With some children, particularly preschool children, mentally retarded children, autistic children, and any others who have difficulty in understanding the response required of them, it may be necessary to *physically structure their limbs, body, and actions* and otherwise prompt them to perform the response. For example, in teaching a small child how to use scissors, one would physically structure the response by placing the child's hands appropriately around the scissors and moving them so as to cut paper. After the physical structuring, the reinforcer is given. After a while (and with some children many trials may be necessary), the child should begin to "catch on" to what is required of him and learn that the reinforcer will be a consequence of his response. In passing, it is interesting to note that when an infant first learns to use a spoon, the whole sequence of operant conditioning events usually occurs. The initial cue each time is the food on the plate, while the operant response is loading the spoon and moving it from plate to mouth. The reinforcement is the food itself which the child enjoys, and in this case it is ideally contingent as a reinforcer because it is a direct consequence of the response action. Physical structuring, prompting, and training have a big part to play in many practical skills and task-learning situations. Note that as the child learns the nature of the response, the physical structuring and prompting can be gradually faded out, until finally the child performs the whole response independently.

## Imitation and Modeling

One of the quickest and easiest ways of enabling a child to understand the response he is to learn is to build it by *demonstrating or modeling the actions* or verbal responses required. For example, if you wish a little child or a mentally retarded child to stack blocks, a simple demonstration of how to do it may be sufficient for him to get the idea. His response should always be suitably reinforced. The modeling of responses or their physical structuring by the intervener is a far superior technique for training a child in required responses than the usual trial and error method adopted by most parents and teachers. Children can be trained positively to perform tasks in the most correct and efficient way, and this often eliminates many problems in the home and classroom (see next definition).

## Task Analysis

A very useful preparation stage for the intervener, when defining a response, is to analyze the exact nature of the task and any sequence of component events which occurs within it. For example, a task analysis of an infant feeding himself would reveal a certain way of holding the spoon, loading the spoon, bending the arm and moving the hand to the mouth, and finally removing the food from the spoon with the mouth. Another situation which requires considerable task analysis is that of a child dressing himself. A task analysis of taking off socks will reveal that even a very small boy or girl can remove a sock by running a finger down behind the ankle bone on the inside of the foot in order to ease the top half of the sock over the heel. One mother with a son named Martin frequently became upset because he would never set the table correctly. "I said to Martin many times," reported Mother, "if you cannot set it properly I might as well do it myself in the first place, but it makes no difference." When Mother was asked if she had ever *repeatedly* shown Martin how to set the table *step by step* (a task analysis), if she had ever thanked him and praised him for setting the table, and if even nowadays she occasionally and happily shared setting the table with him, her answer was "No". Once all these positive facets were brought together into a reinforcement program, the situation soon changed for the better. A task analysis is very important in the case of these types of physical skills because until we have *analyzed* the components and sequence within a task, it is not easy to carry out the reverse process, which is to *build* it as a skill behavior in our children. Of course, task analysis applies to all situations and school subjects. Even a programed textbook is no more than a thorough task analysis of the subject in question.

## Satiation

Say we have set up a schedule for reinforcing Betty with cereal and she has already consumed a large number of Fruit Loops. Then we would say she is satiated and the primary drive is, for the moment, no longer of use as a specific reinforcer. In other words, she is not hungry and therefore, cereal will not be effective as a reinforcer. In this instance, *satiation* means that Betty is not hungry for cereal. However, the individual may still be susceptible to types of reinforcers other than those satisfying hunger; for example, social reinforcement or even thirst-quenching beverages.

*Reinforcement Seeking and Manipulation*

If the reinforcement is a powerful one for a particular person, not infreqeuntly the phenomenon of *reinforcement seeking* occurs.

OFFICIAL CONTRACT

Whereas I, Lynne am a member of this Household I do hereby agree that each evening after supper I will clear the table of dishes etc, without fail [excepting illness].

Whereas I, Maryl am the mother of Lynne I do also agree to award Lynne twenty (20) points without fail for each clearing of the table. Signed: Lynne

Maryl

Witnessed: Robin

Date: 7/7/77

Human beings are an intelligent species; that is, they can understand the *principles* on which things work. It does not take much intelligent insight to understand and remember for future reference that the reinforcement will follow if the operant response is performed. Many species are capable of such insight behavior, especially when a primary reinforcer such as food or drink is the essential objective of the behavior. A pigeon presses a lever in order to get a grain of corn, and a monkey with an electrode embedded in a pleasure center of his brain will continuously press the switch that operates it. Thus it is not surprising that in a highly verbal species such as the human race, a child will turn the reinforcement situation into an established contract and say, for example, "If I pick up my toys, will you give me a candy, please". This situation requires further analysis as there are several answers to it.

1. If Timothy has deliberately spread out the toys in order to get a candy, he is turning the operant situation upside down because the scattered toys become a cue for the mother, the giving of candy becomes her operant response to the child, and Tim's picking up of the toys and putting them away is a reinforcement to the mother. This is called a *manipulation* of the operant conditioning behavior setting; in this instance, Tim is manipulating his mother. This is not uncommon and the best way to handle it would be as follows: Mother says, "No Tim, you may not have a candy because you deliberately spread the toys to get one. I shall now pick up and put away all the toys and I shall have the candy." This should effectively extinguish this specific manipulative behavior within a few trials.

2. If Tim has been *genuinely playing* with the toys and the time has really come to put them away, then in order to *prevent* possible future manipulation and because the time would seem to be right, Mother should introduce strong social reinforcement which is in part verbal and in part her own presence. Thus, Mother would herself *happily help* Tim clear up the toys, all the while saying, "You are a good boy, Tim, to put away your toys," or words to that effect. If, over several trials, Mother keeps on with the strong praise and *gradually* withdraws her own presence from the situation and also gradually withdraws the candy over several days (for example, by substituting drinks and slowly fading them

out), then within several trials Tim should be putting away his toys himself on social reinforcement only. Helping him *occasionally* will maintain the behavior indefinitely, but the helping must be *happy*.

3. One of the simplest ways of handling the toy/candy situation is to recognize the contract *overtly* and put it on a formal basis. This would only apply to those behavior settings in which the child was not manipulating the mother. (If manipulation occurred, she should resort to the plan in paragraph 1 above.) Under the contract system, she would say "Yes, you may have a candy, Tim, every time you put away your toys after you have been playing with them for (state number) minutes." Mother is then back in the situation of teaching Tim good habits by insuring that not only does he put away the toys for the candy, but he occupies himself constructively for ten minutes or whatever the designated time may be. Always remember that boredom is the enemy of learning, so do not defeat your own training programs for your children by having them play with toys or work with materials which bore them. Most toys and school materials cease to interest children after ten minutes' exploration of them. In class, the more boring the work is—for example, learning multiplication tables— the more intensely motivating must the reinforcers be.

## Response Reinforcer (RR) Contracting

This is a formalizing of the contract (abbreviated to RR contracting for convenience) and it can be used to great advantage within the family. A common example of RR contracting is paying children fixed sums of money to mow the lawn, clean the windows, or do the vacuuming. An alternative system to paying out money immediately on every RR occasion is to institute a token economy using a points system. A notebook is kept in which the points earned are entered. The notebook also indicates (in a list) the number of points which can be earned for each separate task. For example, mowing the lawn might be worth 30 points, while filling or emptying the dishwasher might each be 3 points. Make sure that the wage is a fair one or you may have a strike on your hands. A second list in the notebook is a price list, as it indicates what can be purchased with the points. A visit to a movie (or going with friends if old enough) might be worth 20 points, whereas a powered model airplane which flies might be 150 points. RR contracts have great educational value because they teach the child both the value of money in terms of *earning points,* as well as how such an economy "works." Remember that if at any time a child does not wish to earn the money, he has this prerogative under the contract. In such a situation, no force or other interference should be perpetrated by the intervener, as this would be a breach of contract. Note that with children it is wise not to write "long-term" contracts at home involving time, because school is their long-term "contract" in the sense that it is the direct equivalent of adult daily work.

# Chapter IV

# NEGATIVE REINFORCEMENT, AVERSIVE CONTINGENCIES, AND PUNISHMENT

T HERE IS CONSIDERABLE CONTROVERSY in the areas of child care, education, and psychology about negative reinforcement and punishment. Physical punishment is sometimes considered to be cruel or damaging to the personality while deprivations such as isolation are thought of as belonging to old-fashioned mental institutions and prisons. There is no doubt that, in the wrong hands, negative reinforcement and punishment may be harmful, but then that is also true for positive reinforcement or almost anything else in life. Usually, the complete lack of most things would be equally harmful.

Before passing any judgments, it would be wise for us to analyze thoroughly the effectiveness and implications of negative reinforcement and punishment in the home and at school. Although this particular discussion revolves around children, much of what follows is equally applicable to adolescents or adults in penal institutions. As in previous pages, the definitions and explanations given below should give an insight into the nature of negative reinforcement and punishment and how they work.

## Negative Reinforcers

Strictly speaking, a negative reinforcer is any event, the *termination* of which will strengthen or weaken operant responses—that is, *change* them. For example, taking the very commonly used negative reinforcer of spanking, we may note that Alan will stop spitting (antisocial behavior) to avoid spankings (negative reinforcer) if they are applied every time the spitting occurs. Again, a child will sit quietly at the dinner table (acceptable social behavior) in order to avoid spankings. In practice there are several discrete

41

types of negative reinforcement, each of which requires defining separately.

## Withholding Gratification and the Deprivation of Privileges

Any reduction of a *usual* pleasure is a negative act on the part of the intervener. If a child watches television every night for, say, two hours and obviously obtains gratification from his viewing, any reduction on that two hours (which is *not* a reinforcer when it is not contingent upon a response) is a withholding of gratification. *The withholding of gratification can be a matter of degree.* We might say to David that everytime he shouts or screams during the day, his television viewing time will be *reduced* by five minutes. Thus, the reduction of television time (withholding gratification) is now contigent upon the antisocial behavior of shouting or screaming. In the home and in the classroom, the withholding of gratification can be a powerful management system. In the authors' *Motivation Management Materials* each child automatically gets a fixed number of points as a reinforcement for good behaviors, but these are progressively *withdrawn* for the equivalent antisocial behaviors. For example, the child receives points for working quietly but is fined points for being excessively noisy.

## Overpunishment and Excessive Negative Reinforcement

When using withholding of gratification techniques, the intervener *should be careful not to overdo* the negative reinforcement. Most parents, for example, will take away a whole evening's television viewing for one small misbehavior. This is the equivalent of the traffic policeman or a judge fining you $500 for speeding instead of $15. Therefore, always use *small* reductions when withholding gratifications and insure that the child does not turn to substitute pleasures. Note also that there is not much point in depriving the child of twenty minutes of television if he becomes highly absorbed during that time with a fascinating comic book. *Do not overpunish.*

## Ignoring Misbehavior

Some unacceptable behavior (but by no means all) is perpetrated by the child for the major purpose of attracting attention to himself from his peers and adults in the behavior setting. Even in the adult world, notoriety is a factor in the psychology of some criminals, particularly those criminals who say it is. Sometimes the child who cannot get attention any way (this implies a social need for attention in all of us) will resort to misbehavior to attract it. Even the *punishment* of the misdemeanor, if public, may attract still more gratifying attention to the child. Thus, in an upside-down kind of way, the "crime" pays off because in a very real sense the fussing attention of the intervener and any punishment which is public together become gratifying *positive* reinforcers satiating the need for attention. One technique which is sometimes effective with these children is that in which the intervener completely ignores the misbehavior through turning away in a very deliberate way. No direct punishment is meted out, as this would be positively reinforcing. The ignoring tactic on the part of the intervener is a negative reinforcement because it is a *reduction* of an attentional gratification which the child, from numerous experiences, has come to accept as a standard reaction to his misbehavior on the part of the adult. In both classroom and the family, the reaction to attention-seeking misbehavior should be one of ignoring it.

It is a wise move to try ignoring misbehavior as a first-step tactic in any program of negative reinforcement you may be planning. One very important point should be made with respect to ignoring misbehavior. Most research shows that during the first few trials in which ignoring is taking place, *the child may increase the level of his misbehavior* in intensity, duration, variety, or direction in order to have the teacher respond (operantly) with abuse and punishment so that the (reinforcing) attentional gratification is forthcoming. When the child cues the teacher, through misbehavior, to respond with attention, that child has operantly conditioned the teacher, because after the punishment (teacher's response) the child's attentional needs have been satiated so he then, in his turn, reinforces the teacher by desisting from the misbehavior—until his needs for attention build up the next time.

## Time-out Techniques

Time-out brings us one more step in our steady progression down the ladder of negative reinforcement. Time-out procedures involve the removal of the child from all current sources of gratification from which it is possible for the intervener to separate him. For example, by sending Helen into her bedroom for ten minutes for scribbling on her storybook, the parent separates her from television, talking to other people, and all the other satisfactions that may come from the family's behavior setting. (Some authorities call this "time-out *from* reinforcement," but most social contacts or personal pleasures (a) are not contingent upon specific behaviors and (b) are not reinforcing any behavior. Therefore, to say that each specific pleasure such as watching TV is reinforcing is misleading.) Time-out is a complete withholding of *gratification* in order to reduce, extinguish, or build a specific behavior. As a withholding of gratification, it is a punishment or negative reinforcer. An example of *building* a specific behavior through time-out would be *not* sending a child to his room for ten minutes every time he *did* do the dishes. (This is not a recommended practice). In the authors' experience, time-out is one of the most effective methods of negative reinforcement. Here again, five or ten minutes of time-out is usually enough to reduce effectively most anti-social behaviors. Teachers and parents should avoid sentencing children to overlong periods of time-out because in the long run, a child frequently becomes adjusted to solitude and adopts gratifying alternative behaviors such as daydreaming, masturbation, talking to himself, or even sleeping. To be consistent, the intervener *should always use a kitchen timer, to set the time-out interval.* Incidentally, it is a good idea to reinforce the child *after* the completion of his time-out phase if he has behaved well during time-out. If such a positive reinforcement is given, it should almost always be both mild and social in nature. The time-out location can vary according to the nature of the misdemeanor. A very mild time-out would be having the school-age child sit on a chair while he counts out loud up to twenty or fifty. A severe time-out would be fifteen minutes in a relatively bare room. Time-out can be a useful backup negative reinforcement to ignoring misbehavior; that is, when ignoring fails as a technique after a fair number of trials, introduce time-out procedures.

## Aversive Reinforcement

The popular term for aversive reinforcement is "punishment" and the key ingredient in it is pain or discomfort. In all situations of aversive control, the intervener makes pain or discomfort contingent upon the operant response. Note that in aversive reinforcement, the "pain" or "discomfort" may not necessarily be physical because sarcasm, nagging, or shouting at a child also fall into the aversive category. Therefore, from the psychological point of view, aversive reinforcement ranges from mild disapproval to abusive shouting, while on the physical side the range would be from a light tap on the arm to a severe beating. Aversive reinforcement raises many questions pertinent to the emotional development of children and these will be discussed later on a wider basis in a separate section below.

## Natural Aversive Reinforcers

Fester (1967) suggests that much more use should be made of the natural aversive reinforcers which occur in the environment. Examples are putting on dark sunglasess to avoid the pain of strong sunlight, putting on a raincoat to avoid getting wet. Usually, in the case of natural aversive reinforcers, there is more than one operant response which will avoid the full consequences of the reinforcement. Thus, to avoid getting wet in the rain we may (a) put up the umbrella (b) put on a raincoat (c) run very quickly for shelter, or (d) even hold a newspaper over our heads. Two centuries ago Rousseau, in his book, *Emile,* said that one of the best ways to educate a child was to allow him to feel the natural consequences of his actions. Certainly, much more use should be made of natural aversive reinforcers.

## Aversive Social Reinforcement

Fester is also responsible for describing aversive social reinforcement which would include aversive verbal behavior such as mild disapproval and reprimands all the way to loud, angry, verbal abuse. Note that neither Fester nor the authors recommend loud, angry, verbal abuse. Fester would also include withholding gratification (as mentioned above) in this abusive social reinforcement category. The usefulness of the concept of aversive social reinforcement is in contrasting it with natural aversive reinforcers, the latter being preferable when it is possible to use them. Too many parents protect their children from the natural consequences of their actions even when the child is not in danger. A good example of a natural consequence is the young boy who sneaks one of his father's cigars, smokes it, and is sick for twenty-four hours. One such boy named Jack has never smoked since, even though he is now a middle-aged man.

### Escape Conditioning

This is another term used by almost all learning theorists. Escape conditioning is negative reinforcement in the sense that the subject learns to *avoid* the negative reinforcement by responding (or not responding) to a given cue. For example, when John swears (the cue) at David, David does not swear back (operant response) in order to escape time-out (the negative reinforcer). In the final analysis, escape conditioning, aversive reinforcement, and punishment are different aspects of and terms for, an identical process (see note at end of chapter).

### Building Acquired Negative Reinforcers Through Pairing

If the teacher or mother frowns severely each time she punishes a child, the frown, because it is paired with the chastisement, soon acquires a negative power in its own right. Not infrequently thereafter, the frown alone will "nip in the bud" an emerging misbehavior. For example, Paul may be halfway toward snatching a pencil from another child when he notices the frown on the face of the teacher, a sight which stops his hand in mid-air. A tap on the top of the forehead with a finger can be paired with spankings and the tap rapidly becomes a satisfactory substitute for spankings, especially in public places. A wagging of a finger each time a child is left in time-out soon checks unacceptable behavior in its own right, by association. These acquired negative reinforcers may rapidly become initial cues as well, in that the child makes a response by desisting from his behavior and the intervener then positively reinforces him with both praise and a warm "Thank you." Of course, an occasional backup with the real negative reinforcer will be necessary intermittently to insure that the pairing does not weaken (see also the final paragraph of Ch. VI).

## A General Discussion of Negative Reinforcement

For many years, negative reinforcement, particularly in the form of physical punishment, was heavily frowned upon by most educators and psychologists. However, over the last few years, the value of the *judicious use* of negative reinforcers has been rediscovered. The word "judicious" is to be emphasized because unthinking, indiscriminate punishment usually does far more damage to children (and for that matter, adults) than it does to rehabilitate them. However, children have been "cured" from banging their heads to a bloody pulp through the use of mild electric shock, and time-out rooms are now widely used as a part of the treatment of some emotionally disturbed children. If one uses negative reinforcement techniques, one thing is certain: if the program is to be effective, the aversive measures must exert a more powerful negative influence (to escape) than the attractiveness or need-value (payoff) which the behavior in question holds for the individual. For example, if Jane is stealing money and we wish to extinguish this behavior in her, then the value of the money to Jane must be much less than the fear of the punishment she would receive if caught—unless she wants to get caught for the notoriety involved.

It has been said that positive reinforcement is better than negative reinforcement because the former tells the child what he should do, whereas negative reinforcement makes no comment on what his actions should be. This is only partly true, because as defined above, both positive and negative reinforcers can be used to tell the child what he should or should not do. For example, when Father rewards Ralph with a candy for not swearing, this in no way tells the child what he should say when he is annoyed. Likewise, if Ralph is put in time-out for swearing, he is no wiser as to what he should say. If Gordon is told he will be fined a quarter if he does not clean his shoes, the behavior setting spells out very clearly what his action must be even though a fine is a negative reinforcer. Admittedly, it is much better to give him a quarter for cleaning shoes, while the best situation of all is probably a contract.

From what has just been said, it becomes clear that it is not the positive or negative reinforcement which tells a child what he should do but the nature of the behavioral *act* itself. If the behavior itself is *constructive* or socially desirable, then reinforcement of either kind will confirm to him that that is what he should do in future. If the behavior is negative, no amount of positive reinforcement (when he does not do it) is going to present him with an alternative desirable behavior to model, except perhaps by implication.

Once again it is worth stressing the point that the major contribution of behavior modification and operant theory is to emphasize reinforcing positive behavior positively instead of reinforcing negative behavior negatively in the traditional pattern.

As will be seen in Chapter VI, in the authors' experience, negative reinforcers can be extremely valuable when used sparingly *in combination with* positive reinforcement.

## A Technical Note About Positive and Negative Reinforcement

TRADITIONAL DEFINITION OF A POSITIVE REINFORCER. Traditionally, any operants (subjects—animal or human) may "produce" (bring about by their response) reinforcers. If as a result the operant responses *increase* in frequency, then the reinforcers are termed *positive* reinforcers (Bijou, 1961). For example, John may *produce* cookies (through his mother), and if as a result his operant responses of saying please (as a part of his request) increase in frequency, then the cookies can be labeled (by definition) as positive reinforcers.

TRADITIONAL DEFINITION OF A NEGATIVE REINFORCER. On the other hand, any operants may remove, avoid, or terminate (that is, *obviate*) certain (other) reinforcers. If as a result, the operant responses *increase* in frequency, then the reinforcers are termed *negative* reinforcers (Bijou, 1961). For example, John may avoid a spanking (from his mother), and if as a result his operant responses of saying please increase in frequency, then the spanking can be labeled by definition as a negative reinforcer. Taking into account all the variables, the traditional viewpoint can be summed up as in Table I.

TABLE I
TRADITIONAL VIEWPOINT OF OPERANT CONDITIONING

| A | B | C | D | E |
|---|---|---|---|---|
| Operant | Response (Behavior) | Response is Strengthened (Increase); Weakened (Decrease) | Operant Produces or Obviates* Reinforcer | (+ or —) Valence of Reinforcer |
| I John | Saying Please | Strengthened | Produces cookie | (Produces) Positive |
| II John | Not being abusive | Strengthened | Obviates spanking | (Obviates) Negative |
| III John | Not saying Please | Weakened | Obviates cookie | (Obviates) Positive |
| IV John | Being abusive | Weakened | Produces spanking | (Produces) Negative |

*Obviates* is a valuable word in this context, as its meaning covers such terms as avoids, removes, eliminates, decreases.

The authors find this viewpoint semantically and empirically confusing because the terms "positive reinforcer" and "negative reinforcer" have no empirical meaning unless they are qualified with the words "produces" or "obviates." If the terms are not thus qualified, then John is being *positively reinforced* (Column E), whether he says please or does *not* say please (Column B). Bijou (1961) states the following: "The second class, stimuli which tend to strengthen responses that remove, avoid, or terminate them, are called negative because they involve a *subtracting* [Bijou's italics] operation, and reinforcing because the behavior causing this removal is strengthened." Just prior to this, Bijou says, "The first group, stimuli which strengthen the behavior they follow are called positive because they involved an adding operation and reinforcing because the behavior producing the stimulus is strengthened."

Under these definitions, how does one classify "not giving a cookie." If it is a *"subtracting* operation," then it is a negative reinforcer. But according to Table I Line III, "Obviates cookie" is classified as a positive reinforcer. Common sense would suggest that "not giving a cookie" is a subtracting operation and therefore should be labeled a negative reinforcer. By the same reasoning, "not spanking a child" would become a positive reinforcer. Bijou

(1961) indicates that reinforcers are *only* initially identified as positive or negative in operant behavior settings which *increase or strengthen* the response as in Lines I and II on Table I, and by implication the reinforcers so labeled retain their classification in other operant behavior settings such as in Lines III and IV.

The labeling dilemma arises from the fact that any *one* operant behavior setting always contains *two* possible alternative responses (performing the act or *not* performing the act), and *two* contingent alternative reinforcer "consequences" (producing the reinforcer or obviating the reinforcer).

The problem is further compounded in those behavioral settings such as when a child indicates that he prefers (as reinforcement) to receive a spanking rather than be denied a cookie. In other words, the denial of the cookie is for him a more painful *negative* state than the negative reinforcer itself (spanking). Obviously, the cookie itself must be a very powerful positive reinforcer when "produced" by the child's act. But it seems almost contradictory to call "denying the cookie" a positive reinforcer in the above situation. When a man is incarcerated in jail (or a child is in time-out) he has denied himself his free, everyday enjoyment of life. Obviating freedom is by definition a positive reinforcer, and if one is to be logical, so must be going to jail, for the two are the same. Or, should both be labeled negative reinforcers?

In terms of valences and semantics, the problem can be clarified by also giving a valence (positive or negative) to the effect the operant (person) has on the reinforcing (stimulus) environment. Producing is a positive adding effect (plus E) whereas *obviating* is a negative subtracting effect (minus E). Therefore, producing a cookie is a "plus E plus R" (R = reinforcement). Obviating the cookie is a minus E plus R. Producing a spanking is a plus E minus R, and obviating a spanking is a minus E minus R (as we all know from algebra, this is a mathematically and factually positive result because two minutes make a postive). An example of the last case would be to say that to *avoid* a spanking is *not unrewarding*.

Part of the difficulty comes from the implicit assumption that positive reinforcers are always above a zero or "neutral stimulus" line while negative reinforcers are below that line as in the following diagram.

## DIAGRAM 1

Negative          Neutral          Positive

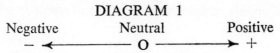

This assumption gives a reinforcer (positive or negative) and *absolute* valence value for a given individual in a specific operant behavior setting. Perhaps the more realistic valency value system is that shown in this diagram.

## DIAGRAM 2
Positive

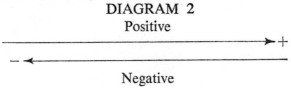

Negative

This is more like the stock market system because it allows for both positive and negative *effects* on *one* operant and in terms of one actual reinforcer. In the case of the stock market, it is the cash value of the shares held by the individual and in terms of cookies, it is whether they are produced or obviated by the operant. However, the present usage of the terms "positive reinforcement" and "negative reinforcement" is very widespread. For example, strictly speaking, *spanking* is *not* a negative reinforcer—it is *obviating spanking* which by definition *strengthens* the response (Table I, Line II) and is therefore the negative reinforcer. *Receiving* a spanking (as a reinforcer) will almost always *weaken* an operant's response and thus contradicts the traditional definition. Even so, almost everyone speaks of spanking as a negative reinforcer, probably because subjectively it "hurts" whereas a cookie is a positive reinforcer because it "gratifies." A child who does *not* respond "correctly" and who thus contingently obviates his cookie certainly views his loss of the cookie as a punishment. Again, if a child *does* respond correctly (in another setting) and he is not spanked he views this as a *gratifying* escape; he is "relieved." He considers he has *not* been punished.

This "operant-oriented" approach takes into account (a) the subject's final state of comfort and discomfort, (b) whether or not he responds correctly, and (c) whether he produces or obviates the reinforcer. It also recognizes that an intervener, experimenter, or environmental circumstance exists in the operant learning situation.

The details of this operant-oriented reinforcement system are set out in Diagram 3.

## DIAGRAM 3

### *OPERANT-ORIENTED REINFORCEMENT MODEL*

*Operant's gratification zone*

Gratification increases in direction of arrows.

Gratification reinforcement—increases strength of correct response (CA) and decreases strength of incorrect response or act (IA).

Operant/Intervener behavior settings (correct act):

1. Gratification level of reinforcement (GR) selected by intervener* and *awarded* to operant for correct operant act (CA).
2. Punishment pain level (PP) reduced or removed by intervener* and not inflicted on operant for correct act (CA).

Operant/Intervener behavior settings (incorrect act):

Punishment reinforcement—increases strength of CA and decreases strength of IA.

1. Gratification level of reinforcement (GR) *withheld* by intervener* and deprivation *pain* inflicted on operant for incorrect operant act (IA).
2. Punishment *pain* level (PP) selected by intervener* and inflicted on operant for incorrect operant act (IA).

Pain level increases in direction of arrows.

*Operant's pain or discomfort zone*
*Or other environmental circumstances.

The reader will notice that the words "positive" and "negative" have been dropped altogether because they are too ambiguous. The terms "gratification reinforcement" and "punishment reinforcement" have been introduced. Note that the latter are not substitutes for the former. Also, the terms "correct act" and "incorrect act" in no way refer to morals or ethical standards. For example, when Oliver Twist (operant) was praised (gratification reinforcement) by Fagan (intervener) for stealing (response), the stealing was a "correct act" (CA) in that particular behavior setting. This system (Diagram 3) is compatible with the viewpoint that the mores, customs, and ethics of individuals and groups are relative. The model presented in Diagram 3 takes into account that a correct act and an incorrect act are exact behavioral counterparts. Examples are politeness and impoliteness, sunbathing and not sunbathing, watching television and not watching television, good table manners and poor table manners, reading and not reading. The reader (or intervener) is free to ascribe to each pole of each pair his own (relative) value judgment as to which is correct and which is incorrect.

Some behavioral psychologists will disapprove of an operant-oriented reinforcement (OOR) model. It makes the impact on the operant the pivotal factor in defining reinforcement. The strengthening or frequency of the response is still just as important in this OOR system but strength is linked to the "correctness" (as a relative concept) of the operant's response. Weakening of the response is linked with the incorrect response (also relative).

In reading extensively in the literature on operant conditioning and behavior modification, the authors cannot find one instance of an experimenter who did not make a *prior decision* as the intervener as to which act or response of the operant was to be "positively" reinforced as the *correct* one (or *desired* one or *preferred* one or *acceptable* one or some other equivalent phrase). Even in the case of natural and circumstantial environmental behavior settings, it is evident that self-preservation, survival evaluations, and common sense almost always empirically determine which response is the correct one and which (opposing) response is incorrect. Thus, to rub one's hands together when out in very cold weather is a "correct response" which warms one's hands in a gratifying way; that is to say, "warmer hands" is an instance of gratification reinforcement for rubbing one's hands together (CA). Of course, the term "gratification" should not be interpreted in any narrow way and it is certainly not synonymous with any "pleasure principle." Perhaps there is a need for some definitive generic word which would cover gratification, survival, self-preservation, preservation of the species, problem solving behavior, and so forth. Thus it can be seen that experimental research in behavior modification is extremely goal oriented (and in the opinion of the authors rightly so) and this goal orientation should be openly acknowledged and theoretically formulated. The OOR model is a start.

*Chapter V*

# PROGRAMS, SCHEDULES, AND PRESCRIPTIONS

As in previous chapters, definitions are the most effective way of describing how we can best adapt our knowledge of positive and negative reinforcement and their concomitants to everyday behavior management requirements. The management of behavior using reinforcement techniques can be extremely effective if a small amount of time is spent in working out specific *programs* to modify, build, shape, reduce, or extinguish behaviors. The more precisely we can define the behavior to be modified and discriminate it from other behaviors, the better our results will be. The selection of a reinforcer and the organizing of its contingency upon the response (the behavior in question or its elimination) must be made with care. Above all, our consistency as interveners in insuring that we reinforce every instance of the response for some time is crucial. Keeping these points in mind, we can now define other important terms.

## Reinforcement Schedules

It is not always necessary once a given response is established to reinforce that response *every time* it occurs in order to maintain it as a response. The following definitions describe various kinds of reinforcement schedules.

CONTINUOUS REINFORCEMENT. This is the situation wherein the response is reinforced at every occurrence. Note that if the continuous reinforcement stops completely, the operant response is rapidly extinguished. Most people would stop work if their wage check ceased permanently to arrive. Similarly, children whose conditioned behaviors are no longer reinforced will quickly stop responding to

54

the cue. Certainly, until the response is well established as a learned habitual one, it should be continuously reinforced.

INTERNALIZED REINFORCERS. There are exceptions to the above rule, namely, when some other reinforcement, usually *internal* to the subject, takes over and automatically reinforces the subject for the response in question. An excellent example of this is reading. While a child is learning to read, it may be quite an effort and therefore, the child will need an extensive program of reinforcement to encourage him to face the problems of acquiring complex decoding and coding skills (reading and writing). Once the child has reached a fair degree of competence in reading, there is a gradual changeover from reliance on external reinforcement (such as praise or, as is unfortunately sometimes the case, punishment) to an *enjoyment* of reading stories or informative articles for their own sake; the enjoyment of the story content is an internal reinforcement. Likewise, a child learning to swim relies less and less on praise and more and more on sheer physical exuberance. Most skills and tasks which have an end other than themselves come into this internal reinforcement category. Therefore, the intervener, when training subjects in skills, should devise a program which allows the external reinforcement schedule to decline in "power" as the internal reinforcement (enjoyment of using the skill for other ends) increases in strength. Always use the continuous schedule of reinforcement when initially establishing a response in the subject. Once the strength of that response has reached a high level of frequency, one should change the reinforcement schedule to an alternative one such as those described below.

INTERMITTENT REINFORCEMENT. Once a response has been well established on a *continuous schedule* of reinforcement, the intervener may wish to switch to a *less frequent or intermittent* reinforcement program. These intermittent reinforcement schedules are found fairly frequently in everyday life. In a sense, our paycheck is intermittent reinforcement when it comes once a week or once a month. Gambling is another kind of intermittent reinforcement in which the payoff usually occurs infrequently. Some chilrend will work for hours or even days on a piece of work such as a drawing, a dress, or a story for a smile and a word of praise from teacher or parent. Many bright children work diligently throughout the entire school year for the intermittent reinforcement of an occasional A grade. Psychologists have defined several types of intermittent reinforcers.

FIXED-RATIO SCHEDULE. This is the term used to describe the reinforcement schedule when the reinforcer is given after a *fixed amount of work* has been completed. This occurs in piecework situations in which the worker receives payment after a fixed number of items or tasks have been completed. For example, some copy typists are paid fifty cents per page and are paid on the completion of every hundred pages.

VARIABLE-RATIO SCHEDULING. Variable-ratio reinforcement simply means that the amount of work to be done between reinforcements is *unpredictable* on the part of the subject. Most parents and teachers operate an unpredictable, variable-ratio reinforcement schedule when it comes to praising the children in their charge. Unfortunately, all too often the giving of praise as a reinforcer depends far too much on the mood of the adult intervener and far too little on the performance of the children.

FIXED-INTERVAL SCHEDULE. If the end of a *time* interval is chosen as the occasion of reinforcement rather than the amount of the response, it is termed an interval reinforcement schedule. The interval is called "fixed" when the interval between reinforcements is a fixed amount of time. For example, when children are reinforced for specific socially acceptable behaviors with a point or token every twenty minutes in the classroom, they are on a fixed-interval schedule. Indeed, this is the type of reinforcement schedule on which most people work.

VARIABLE-INTERVAL SCHEDULE. This term means that the interval between reinforcements is *unpredictable* on the part of the subject—in other words, he does not know when the reinforcement is going to take place in terms of time. In this situation, the response may occur several times during the variable interval without being reinforced. Mothers often unwittingly reinforce whining on a variable-interval schedule. Nick will repeatedly whine for an hour or two to have some privilege, during which time his mother will not give in, until suddenly she "breaks," often just to stop Nick's whining. By agreeing to what Nick wants, his mother reinforces all the whining that has taken place. Nick learns that if he keeps up his whining long enough, he will be able to "crack" Mother and get what he wants. Therefore, his mother should make it a rule that she never accedes to any of his requests unless he uses a "happy" voice. If Nick does not use a happy voice, he has to wait one minute before asking again in a happy voice. Furthermore, to stop him from whining, Nick's mother has a rule that if Nick makes an identical request after it has already been answered (politely) in the negative, he is to go to his room for five minutes time-out each time.

Many mothers who admit they "give in" to their children "just to get some peace" do not realize that this variable-interval reinforcement powerfully *strengthens* the very behaviors they dislike so much in their children. Often, it would be better if they did not say no to the first request. This problem will be dealt with more fully in a later chapter. Note that when building positive behaviors, variable-interval reinforcement works just as powerfully. For the child who is learning to play the piano, an enthusiastic compliment given once in a while by the parents will encourage the child to keep practicing. A husband bringing home flowers or any other suitable gift on a variable-interval schedule will reinforce his wife and make her feel her efforts are worthwhile. Wives should also reinforce their husbands in ways they enjoy.

## Conflict Situations

Several types of behavior settings produce *confusion* and *conflict* in the child or subject and each of these calls for a separate discussion.

1. *Simultaneous positive and negative reinforcement of one behavior*. The parent who says to his child when the child has correctly solved seven out of ten homework problems, "That is good work but you can do much better," is in effect saying that it is good/bad work and the two reinforcers, one positive and the other negative, cancel each other out.

2. *Switching reinforcers prematurely*. Sometimes, teachers or parents start with one reinforcer which is just beginning to work (although the intervener does not realize it) when it is exchanged for another reinforcer. The teacher moves from candy to points, then on to social reinforcement, then back to candy. The children

soon become quite confused, because in a way each switch is a "negative" *withdrawal* of reinforcement as much as it is an introduction of another positive one. Carefully decide on a valid reinforcement program and stay with it for dozens of trials at least.

3. *Conflicting negative reinforcers.* Barbara, who comes to the dinner table on time because otherwise she may be put in time-out, and then has her hands slapped because they are dirty just cannot win. It is up to the parents to separate the two responses (hand washing and coming to the table on time) and program for each its own contingency reinforcement, preferably in a behavioral chain (see later below).

4. *Double response, single reinforcer.* The intervener has to be careful when programing contingencies to insure that a positive reinforcer which is building an acceptable behavior is not at the same time reinforcing another undesirable behavior. Mrs. Guthrie was rewarding her daughter, Sybil, for good behavior in school only to find that Sybil had been lying about her classroom performance.

5. *Conflicting behavior settings.* In this situation, an identical behavior is reinforced positively in one situation and disapproved of in another. This can be very confusing, especially to older children, when no explanations are forthcoming. An adolescent girl will be praised at home for using makeup and wearing clothes which make her sexually attractive, but when she appropriately follows through in a sexual way with her boyfriend, many parents strongly disapprove. We tend to live in a culture in which many parents encourage a sexually attractive appearance but disapprove of overt sexual attitudes and behaviors in their sons and daughters. This can be very confusing to young people, as the high percentage of unwed mothers proves. If sex is with us to stay, then perhaps we have to find less conflicting answers.

6. *Conflicting initial cues.* The above example can be extended to demonstrate how the sexual attractiveness in terms of clothes and makeup of the girl conflicts as a "come hither" cue to the boy, if and when she promptly rejects his sexual advances. Her appearance and expression say "You turn me on," while her speech and immediate actions say "Hands off." In our culture, the culmination of this seduction/rejection conflict are to be found in the Playboy Club Bunny Girl with her physically forbidden, but visually blatant

sex. This is a perfect example of conflicting cues. Some parents and teachers confuse children with contradictory cues. There is the teacher who smiles sweetly while she says "Stay inside during recess and get all those problems right."

## Chaining and Chains of Behavior

Most habitual activities such as smoking are examples of chained behavior. The essence of behaviors which are chained is that the reinforcement of the most recent response is the cue for the next response. In other words, reinforcement and cue become identical, the result being a continuous chain of behaviors running one into the other. One of the best examples of chained behaviors is to be found in the playing of a musical instrument; the sound of the note just played cues us for the next response, namely, striking the next set of keys which in turn contributes to the melody which again in its turn is our reinforcement for striking the notes (response). When an artist builds up a painting, each brushstroke results in a mostly visual satisfaction which in its turn cues him to make the next brushstroke. Even something as mundane as vacuuming the carpets reinforces us in a chain with each clean sweep.

More important for parents and teachers is *language development* which contains a large number of chained behaviors, particularly if the child is reinforced for the production of words both individually and in sentences. Of course, some chained behaviors such as language and walking may also have a strong biological foundation, but this in no way detracts from the importance of their learned characteristics. The development of children can be accelerated and increased in quantity and quality through carefully programed reinforcement all through the years of infancy and childhood. Early stimulation and reinforcement are essential to the growth processes of all children, and their importance cannot be stressed too much.

A good example of chaining in early childhood is to be seen when a child is able to dress himself. Although the sequence in which garments are put on is by no means fixed, it is obvious that socks must be put on before shoes and underclothes put on before outer garments. A child who enjoys getting dressed and who has been carefully taught will follow a set sequence of cue/response/reinforcement *links,* in which each reinforcement success cues the next response. A child who has been liberally praised during the training program when each link was being separately taught will usually be happy to dress quickly and efficiently throughout life. Another example of chaining or chained behavior occurs when a child goes to bed in a routine sequence of behaviors. The alarm or timer rings and the child then (a) undresses, (b) puts on his pajamas, (c) cleans his teeth, (d) goes to the toilet, (e) is tucked up in bed, (f) hears a story, (g) is kissed goodnight, (h) puts out his light, and (i) goes to sleep. This is a complex sequence of interplay between mother and child which the reader may like to analyze in detail in terms of roles, cues, responses, reinforcement and chaining. All the above examples are called *simple chains.*

## Loop Chains

As would be expected, loop chaining signifies that a given sequence of behaviors (or one behavior) is repeated over and over again while the behavior situation holds. Walking (each step) is an example of a loop chain, although some might argue that all species have a biological predisposition to walk. A fully learned loop chain acquired during childhood is the eating of a bowl of cereal with a spoon. The same actions, more or less, are repeated many times until the bowl is empty. Incidentally, eating is an excellent example of a natural reinforcer behavior setting because the pieces of food naturally reinforce the manipulations of knife, fork, and spoon.

## Branching Chains

Almost all the time we are awake, our behavior branches off in a variety of succceeding directions. Because we go in one particular direction at any given moment does not mean that we do not have in our behavior *repertoire* (the sum total of all our learned behaviors) alternative lines of action. What happens is that we zig-zag through the day emitting a very large number of behaviors, each of which is cued by the immediately preceding behaviors, by events in the environment around us, or by events inside ourselves. We "decide" to go to the bathroom rather than to the kitchen for a drink, because nature calls. We "decide" to look at television at home rather than go to the movies, because it is raining. These successive sets of learned behaviors are called branching chains. In children it is possible for the parent or teacher to control the direction of the branching, switching it in desired directions by using appropriate cues.

## Structuring and Scheduling Cues

It can be seen that we should be able to organize much of the behavior of children simply by *structuring and scheduling cues.* Schools have done this for many years with bells to cue the beginnings and ends of lessons. The wise teacher and parent will use all kinds of cues to schedule behavior. The authors have found a *kitchen timer* an invaluable cueing system to signal bedtime, time-out, and television-watching privileges. Thus, it can be seen that the *directions of branching* can be organized by the intervener in sequential programs. Do not think that programing branching schedules by using set cues will destroy creativity in your children. Many people confuse creativity with freedom or license, but in reality the two are not interdependent. Creativity can and must be taught (see below). The genius philosopher Kant, one of the most creative thinkers of all time, ran his personal life like clockwork, and today many writers and artists work a set number of hours each weekday.

## Flow Charting

Just as with the planning of single behavior acquisition, so too can chained behaviors be programed. All we have to do is write down on lined paper (using one line for each "bit") each cue, response, and reinforcer we wish the subject to learn or emit. Add to the sequence any pertinent details and you have a serviceable flow chart. Here is one for five-year-old Mark getting dressed in the mornings. The intermediate reinforcements are pieces of candy that Mark receives on the spot, but which he is to save for eating in the car or bus on the way to school. If he gets completely dressed within ten minutes (set the timer), Mark can also watch television after breakfast.

1. Puts on undershirt (receives a tiny candy).
2. Puts on underpants (candy).
3. Puts on outer shirt (candy).

4. Puts on trousers or playshorts (candy).
5. Puts on socks one at a time (candy).
6. Puts on shoes (candy).
7. Fills pockets with personal necessities (candy).
8. Combs hair (candy).
9. Eats breakfast.
10. Watches television.
11. Eats candy on way to school.

Mark first has to be gently taught with physical structuring that there is an efficient way to put on each of the above items of clothing (for example, turning the socks inside out on the heel). Note that for the purposes of this example, the idea is to train the younger child like Mark to dress correctly in the first place so that he can later reduce this chore to a minimum and get it over quickly. This will give him more time to watch Channel Four (the major reinforcer) before the school bus calls. Of course, *praise* should also be used as an additional paired reinforcer within each link in the chain so that as it is *internalized,* over time he will have an increased personal satisfaction at accomplishing the various dressing skills.

## Writing Prescriptions

In a sense, a prescription is a flow chart, with all possible additional information, which will guide us when we wish to establish the behavior, reduce it, or even extinguish it in a particular individual. A flow chart is more of a general formula, whereas a prescription (as in medicine) is more of a personal thing. Almost all the practical examples given in this book are behavior modification prescriptions.

## Evaluation

In Chapter II, the technique of establishing a baseline of the incidence of the initial behavior was described, as well as a technique for charting the changes in behavior over time by making regular observations each day. As time goes on, it is essential to *evaluate* the progress made each day to insure that our intervention through operant conditioning is effective. The continuous reinforcement program should continue until the required behavior occurs *at least* 80 percent of the time whenever the initial cue occurs. The other 20 percent (if 80 percent was our criterion) would be comprised of instances of the old behavior, no behavior, or distorted versions of either old or new behavior all occurring when the initial cue manifested itself. Ideally, as for example with nail biting, we would wish the old behavior to be eventually 100 percent eliminated or extinguished.

## *A General Discussion of Programming and Scheduling*

The following is a checklist of the points and methods to keep in mind when planning to intervene in any individual's behavior patterns.

1. Try to keep records of all kinds right from the beginning until the new behavior is effectively modified according to the prescription. Obtain baseline data from observations (see 7 below).

2. Carry out a task analysis of the old behavior (if any) and decide at which point the intervention should take place. For example, if a child is not dressing himself properly in the mornings, task analyze the dressing procedure to find where the hold-ups are, such as the inability to put on socks or do up buttons.

3. Draw up a flow chart of all the necessary events required to establish a complete sequence of new behaviors and insure that each link in the chain has its clear-cut initial cue, operant response, and reinforcer. Strengthen weak links.

4. Train the child through modeling, physical structuring, and verbal instructions (of a friendly kind) until he can competently perform each behavior required.

5. Be very consistent and methodical and keep to the flow chart as closely as possible, always insuring that the reinforcement is *immediately* contingent on the response

6. Eliminate all trial and error behavior *because failure is, quite simply, incorrect learning.* The best way to learn is to have success at every stage of the flow chart.

7. If possible, make regular observations and tally specific behaviors on a regular schedule. The frequency of the observations should be determined by the frequency of the original baseline behavior. For example, if shouting tends to occur several times within one hour, then one half-hourly observation at a fixed time of

peak frequency should be sufficient each day in order to log or tally each shout. If we are establishing a new behavior, the frequency is the number of times we would wish it to occur during the day. In place of shouting, we may wish to establish the new behaviors of friendly play and polite requests. If it seems reasonable that these should also eventually occur at a rate of several to the hour, then a half-hourly observation (it could easily be the same one as is used to log shouting behavior) should suffice for counting instances. If possible, keep a graph of the decrease or increase in the required behavior (or lack of it) as this will aid in our evaluation.

8. Evaluate the results on a regular observation time basis, but do not change from a fixed schedule of reinforcement to an intermittent one until after the specific behavior is 80 percent established.

The following two charts illustrate how it is possible to record changes in the frequency of specific behaviors in a very simple way. Chart I is a graph indicating the decrease in a behavior such as

CHART I

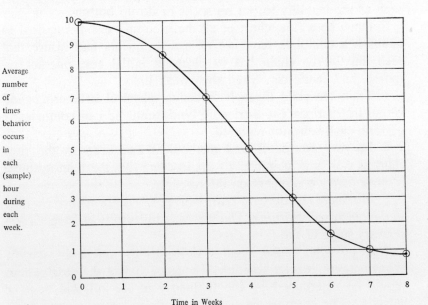

DECREASE IN NAIL-BITING BEHAVIOR

CHART II

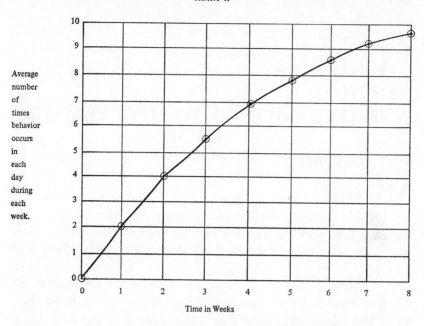

INCREASE IN SAYING "THANK YOU" BEHAVIOR

nail biting which is to be extinguished. Chart II illustrates the acquisition of a new behavior such as saying thank you as it increases in frequency across observations.

If you do not feel you wish to chart the increase or decrease of behaviors in graph form, it is sufficient to write the number of observed behaviors (within the observation period) each day on your calendar so that you can quickly check whether or not the behavior's frequency is steadily increasing or decreasing according to the program objectives. If even this type of limited recording is beyond you, do *not* give up behavior modification as a positive way of managing children and of helping them toward a happier and more rewarding life.

The next chapter describes in some detail a whole philosophy of positive training, including a training for creativity responsibility, industry, and a satisfactory emotional adjustment to life.

# Chapter VI

# THE TECHNIQUES OF POSITIVE TRAINING AND TEACHING

## What is the Need?

M ANY PARENTS AND TEACHERS wish that the children in their care could, through some magic, change their personalities over the days and weeks until they became happy, industrious, kind, courteous, helpful, and fulfilled children. Often, the adults who look after them are perplexed, anxious, and frustrated over their powerlessness to alter the situation for the better. Such parents and teachers *want* to do the best for their children and to bring them up in the "right way," and they feel a real need for solid information on practical child rearing. It is to such parents and teachers that this book and especially this chapter is addressed. The answer to most child-rearing problems can be summed up in the phrase, *positive training and teaching*.

## What Is Positive Training and Teaching?

In the past, most authorities in the field of child rearing and education have contrasted punishment and discipline with a permissive, liberal, "free-spirit type of upbringing. At one extreme, parents either demanded (with the threat of punishment) complete obedience or (in the manner of A. S. Neil) allowed the child to do much as he liked with considerable license. Few parents or even experts have even stopped to consider the possibility of a third and higher order alternative, namely, *positive training and teaching*. The term "higher order" is used because it combines the best of what is called "discipline" and of "permissiveness" and unites them with a third much more important and *positive concept of actively training children* for a much more fulfilling, rewarding, and creative life. Few would deny that ideally, the life of every human being should be mostly positive in outlook, happy, creative, and one which contributes through service to an enriching life for other human beings. However, the virtues just listed do not suddenly appear or develop of their own accord. The philosophy of "natural goodness" says that if you do not restrict or "repress" a child, he or she will unfold to maturity as a free spirit. But this does not take into account that in real life *children learn all the time.* They *learn* social habits and they *learn* antisocial ones. Children *learn* what they are taught and that teaching may be deliberate or unintentional. For example, a child who is punished much of the time learns, among other things, how to escape punishment, how to punish, and how to be aggressive. So he tends to grow up punishing either those around him or himself—or both.

The overly permissive, very liberal parent or teacher is really saying, "I will allow my children to learn at random anything that happens to come their way." Unfortunately, in our peculiar society the odds are high that shouting, screaming, swearing, cheating, lying, fighting, drugs, unhealthy foods, injuries, stealing, boredom, lack of initiative, and so forth are likely to come their way and be learned. It is these negative qualities that "come the way" of most children in our schools, cities, and suburbs. Permissiveness fails because the child has *learned* that standards of behavior are ephemeral and that parents do not value them highly either.

## The "Ideal" Proportion of Positive to Negative Reinforcement

The answer lies in the ratio of positive reinforcement for desirable behavior to negative reinforcement and aversive control for undesirable behavior. The best proportion of positive reinforcement is approximately 90 to 10. In other words, 90 percent of the time the intervener should be positively reinforcing a child for desirable behavior and only 10 percent of the time should be devoted to "disciplining" the child negatively. In all training situations, positive or negative, some type of reinforcement schedule should be worked out. Since 90 percent of the time we hope to be rewarding desirable behaviors, there is a need to examine again what these positive behaviors are so that prescriptions can be written for their reinforcement.

## The "Dichotomy" of Behavior Patterns

The word *dichotomy* has to be used because there is no other to express the twofold nature of almost all behavior. *Dichotomy* means quite simply the division of anything into two opposed parts. Thus, lying and truthfulness are a dichotomy (or a dichotomous behavior pattern) because one is the opposite of the other even though they both refer to the overall concept of verbal honesty. Now it can be seen that it is much better to positively reinforce truthfulness than it is to punish lying, but very few people deliberately do the former. Another dichotomous pair are temper tantrums and constructive discussion in older children. Again, it is preferable to reinforce positively a child's efforts to discuss his problems constructively (and there are role-playing techniques which help do this, as described below) than to try and beat temper tantrums out of the child. Incidentally, spanking a child for a temper tantrum is an aggressive contradiction. One is "saying" to the child through one's actions, "I am having a temper tantrum to stop you from having temper tantrums." Some dichotomous behaviors are listed below. (They were also listed in Ch. I as an introduction to behavior.)

| Positive Behavior | Negative Behavior |
|---|---|
| kind | unkind |
| generous | miserly |
| giving | taking |
| truthful | lying |
| punctual | late |
| helpful | hindrance |
| diligent | lazy |
| motivated | disinterested |
| happy | depressed |
| humerous | overserious |
| trustworthy | shifty |
| gentle | rough |
| content | anxious |
| peaceful | violent |
| sharing | selfish |

| | |
|---|---|
| enjoys physical contact | dislikes physical contact |
| enthusiastic | stick-in-the-mud |
| obedient | disobedient |
| creative | uncreative |
| problem solving | tantrums |
| imaginative | unimaginative |
| constructive | destructive |
| quick | slow |
| tenacious | stubborn |
| organized | disorganized |
| contributory | parasitic |
| loving | hateful |
| law abiding | criminal |

When a group of parents and teachers were once asked to name a specific behavior in their children, almost all replied in terms of the negative list (which they had not then seen). Of course, parents and teachers do not have this negative approach on their own; society as a whole tends to think mainly in terms of repression and punishment rather than providing opportunities for positive rehabilitation and training. For example, our prisons are extremely negative and contribute little or nothing to the prevention of crime.

Each of the above dichotomous pairs, or any others the reader can think of, should be treated as a pair of behaviors within one combined reinforcement program which is 90 percent positive and 10 percent negative. We would positively reinforce kindness 90 percent of the time and negatively reinforce lying 10 percent of the time. We would positively reinforce punctuality 90 percent of the time and negatively reinforce lateness 10 percent of the time. We would positively reinforce high motivation 90 percent of the time and negatively reinforce disinterestedness 10 percent of the time. We would positively reinforce happy behavior 90 percent of the time and negatively reinforce depression 10 percent of the time. With respect to sadness, which some may regard as a legitimate emotion (and the authors would agree), the intervener should ascertain whether or not the sadness stems from a valid environmental event such as a death, separation, illness, or even missing the school gala day. Certainly, except for some criminal act, no one can lay down any final rules about what is acceptable behavior and what is unacceptable. Each intervener must decide for himself or herself what is desirable behavior and what is undesirable. Actually, it is the variations of opinions in such matters which makes for the rich variety of much human endeavor. Therefore, the classification of various behaviors as in the list above by the authors into acceptable and unacceptable groupings is quite arbitrary and is intended only as a guideline to aid parents, teachers, and students in making their own decisions.

Most of the dichotomous behaviors listed above are not specific, but are rather broad categories. For example, there are many different types of lying or stealing and any individualized program for helping children with these difficulties calls for the modification of very specific and well-defined actual *behaviors*. Ted may be stealing money from the mother's purse whereas Jean is shoplifting, and each of these types of stealing would require its *own* individual prescriptions.

Initially, when introducing a reinforcement program, it is beneficial to insure that the first few trials or reinforcement occasions are *positive*. Do not introduce the 10 percent negative reinforcement aspect of the program until Ted has become acquainted with the value of not stealing. The opposite of stealing is earning money legitimately through *work,* and therefore, Ted should be given the opportunity to earn money fairly *easily* each day. Once Ted has a legitimate "income" of his own, then instances of stealing can be punished by deprivation of a privilege, say television. Of course, restitution of the stolen money or goods is also necessary, but do *not* fine Ted, as this will make him *want* to steal. Usually, stealing is a symptom of a child who is deprived of direct affection and attention, so these relationships are to be encouraged.

It should be understood that the ratio of 90 percent positive reinforcement to a 10 percent negative reinforcement is really an ideal guideline, but a very practical one. Very often, it can be instituted for dichotomous pairs of behavior at the start of a shaping program. However, in the case of *some* severe negative behaviors, such as tantrums in older children (who wreck property), it may be necessary to begin with 90 percent time-out and 10 percent (of the time) positive reinforcement for "discussing the frustrating problem" as this latter behavior will be rare. In other words, initially, the baseline frequencies of the dichotomous behaviors may determine the frequencies of the negative to positive reinforcement ratio. Even so, the objective of the intervener should be to keep the "pressure on" to move rapidly to a 90 percent positive /10 percent negative reinforcement schedule as soon as possible. This can be done once the program is firmly established by phasing out the time-out in JND's (just noticeable differences) until the negative behavior is just ignored, while the positive equivalent is richly reinforced.

## *The Importance of Recognition and the Self-concept*

Almost all human beings have a desire to have others recognize the value of their positive behaviors, the contribution they make to the group effort, and their own intrinsic worth as *needed* individuals. This is nowhere more true than in the case of children in a family. The recognition of positive behavior, contributions, and individual worth through physical and affection-based reinforcers gradually builds in the child a sound, positive self-concept which will form a solid and satisfactory core to his personality for the rest of his life. Children with a positive self-concept (one which comes from reinforcement, recognition, encouragement, praise, and from both parents working and playing *with* children) will develop a sound mastery over most of the tasks presented them at home and at school. They will also develop a true, deep self-confidence which will shore them up when they meet crisis situations or other types of dilemmas in everyday life both as children and adults.

A solid, positive self-concept is fundamentally a set of favorable beliefs about oneself. The child with a sound self-concept *knows* he is competent and able to master situations of all kinds (personal, academic, emotional, physical) within the range of his abilities. Such a child has good feelings about himself. For a boy, the mastery of any problem situation is tied to his masculinity as an *effective* person who can meet everyday challenges purposefully and without an overload of anxiety, despair, or fear of failure. Many children *deliberately* fail (do not attempt to gain success) because they *fear* the terrible letdown should they attempt seemingly difficult tasks in school and sometimes at home.

## Hope, Failure, and Security

It is one of the strange paradoxes of life that often the security of constant failure is preferred to the possibility of success. "If I insure that I fail" says the child (or adult), "then at least, I spare myself the fearful *depressing crash of spirit* which would follow had I genuinely tried and then failed." It takes tremendous reserves of courage to pick up *repeatedly* the shattered pieces of failure and try yet again to achieve success for the umpteenth time. In such circumstances, hope is a fragile web spun and respun in an exposed pathway all too easily torn by heedless teachers and parents. Why try and try again when it's 10 to 1 the result will be a "C" or "D" followed by the inevitable condemnation anyway.

Note that if a child has been raised to have a negative self-concept of any kind (caused by a lack of recognition, praise, encouragement, and so on, and an excess of criticism, punishment, sarcasm, nagging, and so forth), then it may be necessary to use candy or other material reinforcers initially in order to reverse the downward trend. A program such as the *Home Behavior Management Chart* (Bannatyne and Bannatyne, 1970) can usually help bring about a more positive situation which with affection and consistency will lead to a permanent, masterful self-concept. Even the best reinforcement systems become neutral, mechanical devices without a warm, praising, loving relationship between adult and child.

## The Importance of Parent and Child Enjoying Each Other

It is absolutely essential that each parent and child should genuinely *like* each other if that child is to develop positively in personality and academic achievement. Liking is a little different than loving, although of course, loving should include liking. Liking implies really *enjoying* each other (and each other's personality) in a way that enriches both people. All the tokens, points, toys, and other tangible reinforcers can only develop the parent-child (or teacher-child) relationship to a certain point beyond which *attachment* of a personal nature is extremely important.

Although many attachment behaviors (see below in this section) are specific and should often be contingent, there is an essential place in the family for what might be called the "diffuse gratification reinforcement" of liking each other and of mutually enjoying life. In this milieu, the pleasant feelings suffuse the families' relationshops, permeating them with a sense of well-being. This positive atmosphere serves both to *generate* and *to reinforce* desirable behaviors in the children, especially if the parents are aware of the specific behaviors they wish their children to learn.

Note that sometimes a social (attachment) reinforcer can be strengthened (in parallel) by combining it with a tangible reinforcer. A candy *and* a kiss may often be more powerful together as a multiple reinforcer than either would be separately. The attachment behaviors and reinforcers of liking and loving are not some nebulous, qualitative emotion floating between people. They are composed of observable, practical, measurable sets of real behaviors which actually exist between people. These *acts of liking and loving* develop through various types of communication and it is these communications (described below) which have to be examined in detail if one is to learn how much such attachment relationships are built. Remember, if there are no *acts* of love there *is* no love. One cold father would not show much love or direct affection to his children (or wife) because "they might take advantage of it." How warped was his view of life and loving.

## The Importance of Smiling

Many studies of babies and infants have shown that smiling is one of the key natural reinforcers in building atachment bonds between mother and child. Smiling is equally important in the building of friendship and pleasure between other members of the family. Smiling is a signal that one wants to be friendly, and once the friendship is established, smiling continues to strengthen it through mutual reinforcement. Therefore, parents and teachers should smile frequently in a genuine way. Note that a hollow smile is worse than none, as it usually contradicts some other negative action or criticism—for example, the smile on the face of the proverbial tiger or Cheshire cat. Smile at children spontaneously, and for no other reason than that they are there.

## The Importance of Physical Contact

In most modern Western societies, personal physical contact has become much less frequent than it was centuries ago or than it is in some other cultures (e.g. Indonesian). The "don't touch me" syndrome is a complex one, but our society is already to the point where most people apologize if they happen to brush aganist or touch an acquaintance by chance.

Unfortunately, this peculiar fear has pervaded many families. Sometimes the main physical contact between parents and child is one of punishment in the form of pushing, shaking, spanking, and similar action. The association of fear and anger with skin hardly prepares the child for an intimate, loving, and sexual life when he or she grows older. This does not mean that punishment should never involve contact; rather, it means than any infrequent physical punishment must be far outweighed by very frequent gentle attachment contacts.

The forms of positive personal contact are many. Hugging one another is natural and normal as a greeting, at bedtime, as a part of "goodbye," or at times of overflowing joy. Examples of this might be when a child gets a good report card, or does his first somersault on the living room carpet. Variations of the hug should be commonplace in the family. Father's arm around the shoulder of his teen-age son or daughter assures them of his love. Ruffling the hair, back patting, stroking the cheek two or three times quickly, very gentle brief tickling, and even hand shaking should all be a part of one's contact with one's family.

*Not included* are those aggressive-in-fun practices which many fathers and some mothers foist on their children because as parents they are too embarrassed about real affection and genuine, gentle physical contact. These aggressive-in-fun "games" include the pretend punch to the stomach, chest, or jaw, the playful spank or kick on the bottom, the hearty slap on the back (accompanied by a guilty laugh) the pinch on the cheek or pulling of hair. All these specific aggressive-in-fun acts associate aggressive behaviors with attachment contacts, a pairing which is inconsistent and leads to a "you only hurt the one you love" behavior syndrome in adult life.

Romping of a nonaggressive kind is quite legitimate. Here one

must carefully distinguish between aggressive behavior and boisterous activity. In adult life, for example, sexual intercourse may
often be boisterous but not necessarily aggressive. Once children
can swim, a good place for romping is in the water; another excellent place is the family room on a rug or rubber mat.

Kissing and caressing are not just for lovers, and they are not
always sexual. In the morning and at bedtime, kissing is a regular
essential confirmation that the family attachments are solid. A
nuzzle in the neck and a kiss will generate warm feelings in humans
of all ages unless they have been negatively conditioned to react
unfavorably to them.

In concluding this section, it is worth emphasizing yet again the
*importance of positive physical contact* between all the members of
a family. Affectionate contact can be both a behavior to be
reinforced (if it has to be built), or a valuable reinforcer of other
behaviors if it already exists.

## The Importance of Father

If father is not in the home or if he is not interested in his
children's school progress, then quite frequently the children will
lag behind their peers. Boys tend to identify with their fathers—
that is, they often model themselves and their actions on what their
father *is* and does. This attachment provides the father with a key
reinforcer of his son's work habits and behaviors. Most fathers are
only too ready to punish or disapprove of their children's mis-
behaviors. If those fathers would only add to the behavioral mix a
high proportion of praise and affection, within a few weeks they
would see quite dramatic changes for the better in their children's
behavior.

Girls acquire many of their attitudes toward the male sex through
their relationship with their father. If he is afraid of physical
contact with his daughters, if he mostly rejects (negatively
reinforces) their attempts to make contact with him, and if he "puts
down" their growing attempts to be emotionally and sexually
feminine, he will negatively color their future feeling for men.
Many an estranged wife can look back to a father who negatively
reinforced specific feminine feelings.

If a girls' mother reacted in a similar negative way, her fate was almost inevitable. Occasionally, however, a girl will react against her parents' negative reinforcement in adolescence and strive to develop her femininity outside the family in a defiant way; frequently, it is joyless. If a boy or girl is to grow into a mature adulthood, a positive training in attachment and in the ways of femininity and masculinity is essential.

### The Importance of Praising: The Single Most Powerful Reinforcer of a Favorable Self-concept

The key reinforcer in building a child's good opinion of himself and his abilities (his self-concept) is *praise*. Most parents and teachers are not generous enough with praise. They think that praising a child will "spoil" him. Praise or other reinforcers, when contingent on a constructive behavior, can *never* "spoil" a child. What *does* spoil a child is the *random* use of punishment and rein- forcement which is *not* contingent on acceptable or desirable behaviors. A life without positive or negative reinforcers will also usually "spoil" a child. (The word "spoil" is used here to mean that the child acts and behaves very much in accordance with his own whims and wishes and that his behaviors are almost entirely antisocial and self-oriented in nature.) Never call children negative names such as "fool," "dodo," "ding-a-ling," "stupid." One father called his bright daughter a "dodo" all her school life, and she was always depressed because she believed him.

Praise is an extremely beneficial reinforcer which must always be used contingently on desired behavior by parents and teachers. It is quite compatible with all other reinforcers, particularly points and token systems, and can always be used as part of a multiple reinforcement program. There are hundreds of phrases and sen- tences in our language which can be used to praise children. Adults should acquire a wide repertoire of these phrases and strive to use them in context—that is, appropriately to the behavior that is to be strengthened. For example, the sentence "You do have a good imagination," might be used when the child paints or draws any original picture. Do *not* use adult standards to judge a child's work, skill, or performance. Many parents and teachers have standards which are much too high.

## What Should We Praise?

There may be several facets to a particular behavior, as well as different types of behavior, even in the positive range. Each aspect of a behavior will be discussed separately below.

### Praising the Task, Act, or Deed as an End Result

If a child builds a model plane, sets the table, completes a series of mathematical problems, takes out the trash, or does any of a thousand tasks, there is a point when the act or deed is complete and the end result is produced. The model stands in all its glory, the table is fully set, the trash can is back in place and relined, or the mathematical problems all have their answers. The child has been able to do well because the tasks were well within his capabilities and were broken down into success-achievable units. (See earlier section on task analysis in Ch. III.) *The completed act, deed, or task must be praised,* and as has been said previously, that praise must be immediately contingent on the completion.

### Praising the Emotions and Feelings That Accompany the Performance of the Task, Act or Deed

All too often, parents, teachers, and others do not realize the importance of the *feelings* a child has while carrying out the task, act, or deed. If the child is to learn to *like* performing tasks (that is, to evince the right emotions), then the parent or teacher must regularly praise the display of "good" feelings at the times they are shown. It is easy to say "It's nice to see you enjoying yourself," or again, "What a cheerful person you always are." The praising of feelings should never be stilted—rather, it should be as natural and informal as possible and it must be frequent.

When the tasks or chores James has to do are not all that pleasant (e.g. taking out the trash or learning to spell twenty words), it is even more highly desirable to praise the emotions and feelings he has (or should have) shown during the performance of the task. James' mother praised him for his sense of pride in helping her. "You must feel proud of helping me by taking out the trash, James. You *are* a fine son." In the case of the spelling she said, "James, you should feel very pleased with yourself for working so hard at learning to spell those twenty words; you are a diligent lad." "What's diligent mean, Mom?" James asked. "It means you enjoy the satisfaction of working hard to do a job well and to finish it successfully just as you have done—good boy."

## Praising the Skills and Speed Used to Carry Out the Task

The techniques or skills used to perform a task, act, or deed are very important. When the child is naturally efficient or has learned his skills well (in home or classroom), he must be praised. Very often, the analysis of a task into its component parts may produce a set of skills each of which will require reinforcing with praise. For example, Peter, who is learning to write cursively, should be praised for the way he shapes his letters, the spacing of the letters, the way in which he holds the pencil, the evenness of letter height, and so on. In the home, when Ruth sets the table for dinner, she should be praised for the way she carries the dishes safely, the neatness with which she lays the cutlery on the table, the folding of the napkins, the placing of the knife on the right side, and so on. Obviously, it is impossible in any book on behavior to task analyze every behavior or set of behaviors human beings indulge in. However, it is quite easy for the teacher or parent to learn to *observe* behaviors for the purpose of task analyzing them. Reinforce yourself with some little pleasure each time you successfully task analyze a situation.

## Praising Politeness, Friendliness and Other Positive Relationships

Human relationships are every bit as important as practical tasks and once again, it is to be emphasized that relationships such as friendliness and politeness are observable behaviors (just like loving) and that all these *acts* can be beneficially reinforced. If Jerry is praised for saying please and thank you, he will be encouraged to be even more polite in the future. The words "Thank you for saying thank you," may sound strange to an adult but not to a child. Of course, if a child does say please or thank you, he should be immediately rewarded by having the food or other request immediately granted. When Jerry says "Please may I have a cookie, Mommy," and he receives that cookie ten minutes later, he is not exactly being encouraged to say please in the future. On the other hand, it is quite a good idea to make a child wait for one minute (no more) for his cookie (or other request) if he forgets to say please. If the above reinforcement systems are put into operation, a child will be automatically polite before the age of four years.

Friendliness can also be built through reinforcement procedures. In most families, there is considerable sibling rivalry, if not outright fighting. This is best counteracted at an early age, although much can still be done with older children. The key is to reinforce every act of friendliness, sharing or giving between the two children concerned. Even a group of children can be praised frequently for working or playing happily together. The teacher who says to her class once or twice a day, "This must be the best class I ever had, you are all so *friendly* with each other," will have a more contented class than one she continually upbraids for quarreling.

Social skills such as politeness, friendliness, greeting people, telling people how much they are *enjoyed*, helping people without interfering, expressing pleasure in sharing, and learning to praise others are all essential aspects of a positive, well-rounded personality.

## Praising Praising and Other Reinforcing Activities in Children

It may seem strange to talk about praising praising until one realizes that the *act of reinforcing* is just as trainable as any other behavior. It is a good idea to say to children regularly, "You are a kind boy for saying such nice things about your little brother's drawing (or other accomplishment)." In fact, praising the act of "saying nice things about others" should become a stock reinforcer in every parent's and teacher's repertoire. It is very important to the harmony of the family, school, and human society that children be praised or otherwise reinforced for their own acts of reinforcing others. Everytime a child acts favorably in any manner toward another, he must be reinforced for that behavior. Kind acts between children today mean kinder acts between adults tomorrow.

## The Age to Begin

The answer in every case is *now*. Whether the individual is four weeks old or forty years old makes no difference, though in the latter case the change *may* come more slowly. The psychological principle of reinforcement, especially the positive type, is universal and applies to all learning.

Fundamentally, the reinforcement principle says that we like doing those tasks which lead us to satisfaction whether the satisfaction be a direct consequence or simply contingent on the completion of the task. Many wives (and some husbands) have cleaned the house in the expectation of delighted praise from their returning spouse. Everyone likes to be appreciated (reinforced). The wife who is not reinforced for cooking delicious meals will soon give up and serve only easy routine dishes to her family.

In a previous section, the importance of smiling was stressed. Most infants begin to smile sometime between three and six weeks of age, and this attachment response on the part of both baby and mother is the beginning of (hopefully) a lifelong pattern of positive reinforcement. Unfortunately, at some time during the second year of life, many mothers switch from smiling, cooing, and praising their child to an ever-increasing number of "no-no's," threats, shouts, and even slaps. There seem to be so many things which the toddler must learn *not* to do that all too frequently, mothers forget they should be positively training the child to carry out all things he *should do*. For many mothers, the only thing a toddler "should do" is to play with toys quietly in the middle of the floor or playpen. Attempts at exploration, climbing, and similar activities are cut off as being too dangerous. Many mothers do not realize that it is possible to train even tiny infants in quite complex physical skills. One eleven-month-old girl, who had not yet learned to walk easily, learned in *two lessons* of physical structuring how to climb down from a sofa or adult bed by first lying on her stomach, then swinging her legs down and sliding slowly until her toes touched the floor safely. Thereafter, the parents had no fear of her hurting herself by falling off those articles of furniture. "Physical structuring" is of great importance in training children of all ages, but especially in toddlers who cannot yet speak clearly. The ability to imitate is strong and seems built in. If one watches closely, one can observe little children striving to copy every movement they know the adult is trying to teach them. All expressive activities involve muscles, and this is as true of speech as it is of physical acts or means of communication. Thus, the infant will watch closely, then strive to mimic the adult model.

Physical structuring is even more direct than imitation. By the adult's positioning of the child's body and limbs, the child will often learn very quickly the physical act or sequence of acts (task analyzed) which he is being taught. Again, all these achievements must be contingently praised. Even an eleven-month-old baby knows that he has done well when he is hugged, kissed, and praised the first few times he backs down off a sofa succesfully. Older siblings can beneficially join in this praise and other reinforcement.

## Development Factors and Tolerance

Always make the tasks a child is required to perform not only simple and easy in the beginning, but also *well within his developmental range physically and psychologically*. All the reinforcement in the world will not train a child to play a championship game of chess at age four. Nor will it teach an eight- to eighteen-year-old to sit still comfortably for two hours (all schools please note). It is also wise, with the introduction of each new task, to allow a "breaking-in period" during which the child can adjust easily and successfully to the task-reinforcement routine. The keynote of the breaking-in period is *tolerance*. If, for example, a very young child is learning to say please each time he asks for something, the mother should be only positive for the first month or two before introducing the aversive reinforcement of the one-minute-wait each time he fails to say please. The more complex a task is (that is, the more difficult it is to master), the greater is the need for tolerance on the part of parent or teacher. Learning to read or calculate can be an extremely difficult achievement for numerous children who have mild or severe learning disabilities. Adults with negative attitudes (including impatience and irritation) will only systematically associate subjects such as reading and arithmetic with negative feelings, thus turning the child away from those subjects probably for the rest of his life. On the other hand, gentleness, patience, and consistent positive reinforcement over months and *years* will almost invariably bring about a pleasureable academic achievement.

## Praising People in Front of Others: The Importance of Pride

While praising children in a one-to-one situation is always beneficial, the value of praising an individual in front of a group can be even more powerful as a reinforcer. When the rest of the family, class, or team are there to listen, a child positively swells with pride when his mother, teacher, or coach proclaims what an excellent performance that child has achieved. If adults received their degrees, medals, or other symbols of success only secretly in private, the sense of achievement would be more than halved for the recipient. The pride of being praised in public for being successful is universal and seems to be an essential motive for the human race. Certainly, while a child must always be praised individually, so also must he be praised in front of others.

## Role Playing as a Part of Learning

One very effective method of teaching children is to have them act out a particular role or task several times and praise them each time for the successful completion of that task. This technique of role playing with reinforcement can be used in place of negative reinforcement in many instances. A case in point is the child who slams doors to the chagrin of the rest of the family. Such a child should be physically structured as to the best way to close a door quietly (turning the handle before the latch makes contact and then releasing it) and warmly reinforced each time he does this during the training period as well as subsequently. Role playing can be verbal as well as physical. Children can role play sharing their toys and learning to speak politely to one another while playing. Little Robbie quickly learned to share his toys with his baby sister when he was constantly reinforced in a role-playing situation involving toy sharing. He appreciated the point even more when Father shared his "toys" (tools) with his son and pointed out that the whole family always shared their possessions.

Another variation on the role-playing training situation is demonstrated by the case of the older sister (Kate) who did not want to share her chocolates with her younger brother and sister. Kate's father *pointed out that we all share* with each other and that she would soon find out what it was like not to be shared with in other different situations. Fifteen minutes later, Kate wanted to cuddle up to her daddy while they watched TV, but he *gently* pointed out that he did not want to share his sofa with her. She announced that she did not care anyway. Ten minutes later, Kate picked up some toy shears belonging to her baby sister. Father took them away saying that her sister did not want to share her shears with Kate. At this point, Kate got the message, ran to the refrigerator, and distributed *all* the chocolates to *all* the family in a magnanimous gesture; then she cuddled up to her daddy on the sofa (as a reinforcer). Note that this whole episode would not have been as effective without the initial explanation to Kate by her father.

There is no end to the number of situations which lend themselves to role playing, physical structuring, and imitation. The common element in all these learning methods is reinforcement, especially of a positive kind. It is very important to note that reinforcement is as an essential part of the formal learning situation as it is in the rewarding of spontaneous positive behaviors.

## Distraction

With very young children, and *sometimes* with older ones, distraction can be a powerful management technique. The principle is simple. The child is diverted from an undesirable activity by the presentation of a powerful stimulus which will divert the child into another acceptable activity. As a parent or teacher, if you resort to distraction to control children's behavior, be sure that the new stimulus is not "seen" by the child as a reinforcer for the unacceptable behavior. If it is "seen" as a reinforcer, then the original unwanted behavior will be built. Therefore, always vary the use of many distractors across a variety of negative behaviors. At still other times, offer the (distracting) objects as playthings when they are *not* being used as distractors. Thus, any ongoing contingency situation is obviated. *Also, do not use distractors merely to avoid facing the need for a contingency reinforcement program.* Distracting a child from a negative behavior situation may avoid negative behavior in the short term, but it does not necessarily build good behaviors in the long term.

Infants under two years of age usually are best "controlled" through distractions. A boy who has not been eating well will often do so if he has a box of small toys to play with. Two older children may desist from quarreling if the television set is switched on or a game of Monopoly® is suggested. However, with older children, use distraction only as a short-term tactic and rely on behavior-modification programs as a main strategy. Remember too that genuine family activities of all kinds (including work) are not necessarily classified as distractions. Recreation and hobbies have built-in reinforcers in the form of personal satisfactions and they are to be recommended as fulfilling activities in their own right.

## A List of Distractors for Infants

Pull-cord speaking toys.

Shoe box of old pencils, crayons, erasers, etc.

Shoe box of small bottles, brushes, metal dishes, lids, caps, etc.

Shoe box of old costume jewelry (do not include small earrings).

Set of felt-tipped water-ink pens and many sheets of paper (given one at a time).

Cookie tin full of multicolored rubber bands.

Music boxes of all kinds, especially in toy radios and TV sets.

A dish of ten different small seashells.

An old cassette tape recorder with family recordings (on the child's table).

Television (nearby).

Transistor radio (on the child's table).

Singing songs together (especially in the car).

Conducting music together (especially in the car).

Looking at old magazines (the child can turn the pages).

Tiny objects inside small boxes, old ring cases, or baby food bottles which the child can open with effort.

Any toy, such as a windmill or waterwheel, which can be spun by the child.

In fact, any toy or object which moves, which is a puzzle, or which is novel will distract a child. Keep changing the objects so that the child never quite gets bored. Always put the new objects down in front of the child before the old one is taken away. Do not use the distractors as everyday toys. Keep the boxes of distractors on a high shelf and bring them down one at a time when needed.

## The Importance of Parent and Teacher Participation

If one observes those parents and teachers who are successful in teaching, training, and managing children of all ages one soon discovers that such success partially stems from involvement and activity participation by the adults in question.

The father who encourages his children to help him and work *with* him around the house and who plays football, checkers, hot wheels, and other games *with* them is going to have little trouble in terms of negative behavior. The same holds for Mother. Note that both boys and girls can participate in all kinds of activities with both parents. Girls can play football and boys can sew sails on the sewing machine with equal enthusiasm. The teacher who actually takes a character role in a class play will have far fewer discipline problems than the one who merely directs and supervises.

Adult participation is in a sense a powerful positive reinforcer in its own right. Children get happy, pleasurable feelings when grown-ups work and play *with* them. This is equally true whether the activities are on the children's level or on the adult level.

## The Development of Learned Cues and Signals

In the animal world, *signals* are an important facet of controlling behavior. When most animals see a skunk turn around, they run. When a snake coils, it is time to leave the scene. A gorilla howls and beats its chest in a "mock" tantrum to frighten away intruders. Many signals are designed to attract, especially courting and sexual ones. Human beings have many such positive and negative signals and quite a lot of them are learned. Examples are winking, making a fist, scowling, smiling, and making eye contact.

It is quite easy to build signals or cues to which children will respond, thus avoiding the need for following through with some established behavior-modification program. As was mentioned in an earlier chapter, a tap on the head which is associated with a spanking may suffice to check unacceptable behavior. A nodding of the head may substitute for positive praise or reinforcement in a public situation. Traditionally, a wagging finger has checked many a child about to commit a misdemeanor. One teacher developed a system of finger signals to tell any particular child in the group how many points they could give themselves on the wall chart for good work. Parents, teachers, and children can spend valuable time developing a system of signals and cues to facilitate reinforcement programs.

## Uses of a Kitchen Timer

An ordinary kitchen timer can be used as a practical part of many reinforcement programs. Much of adult life is regulated by alarm clocks, traffic lights, telephone signals, and dials of all kinds. The following list of uses for a kitchen timer is a practical one. Compliance with the timer should *always* be positively reinforced.

1. Going to bed. Set the timer to ring at the desired time.

2. Getting dressed before breakfast each morning. Set the timer for ten or fifteen minutes within which time the child has to dress. Positively reinforce success and negatively reinforce failure. Be sure the time interval is fair. On a different type of program, play "Beat the Clock."

3. Sharing toys. Give each child five or ten minutes' individual play with single toys which more than one child wishes to play with, e.g. riding a bike, using a tape recorder.

4. Doing the dishes (or other chores). Set the timer for a maximum reasonable time limit (half an hour?) and for every five minutes less than the maximum it takes to complete the task, award five minutes TV viewing time after the usual bedtime.

5. TV viewing time, or reading in bed privileges, etc. Set the timer to indicate the time allowed; when the bell rings, time's up. Try to match the bell with the end of a TV program.

6. Homework. If you possess a stopwatch (also an excellent cue/signal instrument with many uses), start it off when the child begins his homework and stop it when it is all *correctly* done. Then allow the *exact* equivalent TV viewing time that same evening and use the timer to time the earned viewing time. Note that if the child has little or no homework, then normal TV viewing should be permitted.

7. Clearing up, putting away, tidying room, cleaning anything, etc. Use one of the systems listed above for such tasks. Most often No. 2, 4, or 6 can be implemented.

*Chapter VII*

# QUESTIONS COMMONLY ASKED

*Is Duty a Valid Concept?*

O NE OF THE MOST COMMON questions asked by parents, especially the strict ones, is "Why does a child have to be bribed to carry out tasks which it should learn to do out of duty to others?" This question takes us into a totally different realm of looking at behavior, but it must be answered for the new theories of learning to become established.

What is duty? How is a child *trained* to become dutiful, Does duty occur spontaneously in the human being, and if so why are we all not automatically dutiful?

The main problem with the concept of duty is that traditionally, it has been thought of as a carrying out of tasks for others without asking or expecting any reward. If a reward was ever suggested, it usually took the form of "duty brings its own reward," presumably in some form of self-satisfaction. We suspect that most people who are dutiful are rewarded or self-reinforced through an internalized, rather serious, self-satisfaction. The reason for this is that they have been raised that way by parents who in restrained fashion *praised* their children's dutiful acts. It usually never occurred to these parents that the very same "dutiful" acts could be taught their children in a quite different context than the rather over-serious and teeth-gritting one that we usually associated with duty. By using the techniques described in previous chapters, parents and teachers can effectively bring up children to like doing chores, helping others, being tidy, and having sound personal relationships with other people. To use the old-fashioned term "duty" for these behaviors is an unnecessary misnomer; it is better to dispense with the word duty altogether, for it is commonly thought of as magically appearing in children at a certain age. Remember, children have to *learn* how to help others, and to do so there *must be* some reward, satisfaction, or reinforcement which they receive as fair due. In the early years of childhood, the reinforcement for helping may be candy, points, and praise, but later in life when all these reinforcers have been internalized, the "reward" may be something as intangible as self-development. There can *never* be learning (dutiful or enjoyable) without *some* reward, reinforcement, or payoff, and in the face of the research evidence, anyone who clings to the unrealistic idea that children will work because of *their* love for parent or teacher or out of "duty" is just not aware of the reinforcements occurring in the learning situation. Once, one of the authors asked a housekeeper named Bridie why she was so cheerful whenever she was vacuuming, cleaning, or dusting. She replied, "When I was a young girl in Ireland I always used to help my mother in the house with cleaning, cooking and looking after the younger children. My mother was a gentle, kindly woman and she was always praising me for the work I did in the home. If there were visitors she made me feel very proud by telling them in front of me what a wonderful helper I was, how quickly I worked and how she did not know how she could ever get along without me. You see, my mother was a very good woman and I often think about her."

## Will My Child Become Materialistic If I Use Primary Reinforcers?

The answer to this question is no. In detail the answer has several facets.

Remember that awarding a child toys, points, tokens or even pennies for *work* completed is exactly equivalent to an *adult salary* or wage. If you as an adult were suddenly deprived of your salary in fair payment for a good job of work done would you continue to work for the love of the boss or out of a duty to mankind? It is not materialistic to expect reasonable payment for one's work.

It is also wise to remember that there is nothing contradictory or incompatible about duty, love and wages. Many a teacher, doctor, nurse, clergyman, business man or other worker has a strong sense of duty, compassion and dedication in his or her work as well as receiving a salary. Children or no different.

Quite often in life it is the experience of deprivation that determines a strong need for something. Children who are always hungry become obsessed with food. Children deprived of toys and possessions yearn for them and envy others. It is these *deprived* children who tend to be materialistic. Many of today's young adults who as children were given plenty of everything in a material sense complain that their *parents* are the ones who are materialistic. Allowing children to *earn* toys and privileges makes them very aware of the value of honest work and the work they do need never affect a healthy affectionate relationship between children and parents. If anything, one strengthens the other especially when points are paired with praise and affectionate reinforcers.

## Are There Particular Ages When Specific Functions Are Best Trained?

Although some psychologists still argue as to whether or not there are "critical periods" in the development of children during which specific functions appear, the authors have no doubts that there are.

Most psychological functions in childhood clock-in at particular ages in such a universal way that if they do not do so, the child is taken to a doctor or psychologist for examination to find out why the delay has occurred. If, as some experts claim, language is totally learned, why is a child who cannot speak at four years of age considered abnormal? If he has not learned mathematics at four, he is not thought to be abnormal. Our knowledge of developmental processes is always at odds with our anxiety about training and teaching our children everyday tasks and functions. On one hand, parents ask, "If I let my child develop naturally and normally without interference will he not grow into a natural maturity?" while on the other hand, there is the nagging question, "If I do not teach my child how to live, to have good habits, and how to help others he will become a spoiled brat, is that not so?"

This conflict between spontaneous development and firm training is most clearly seen when the parent is faced with what to do about a child's aggression. Some parents opt for freedom only to find that their children become either tyrants who are always fighting and squabbling and lording it over others, or they become fearful children somewhat anxious in nature. They may also be withdrawn or overwilling to please everybody. Some parents decide that discipline is the answer and that raising children is a *contest* to see who has the better of whom. These parents believe that any type of antisocial behavior which may be exhibited even at an early age must be nipped in the bud and stamped out before it can become a habit. There is a sufficient kernal of truth in this attitude for it to have become well established as a child-rearing technique across many civilizations and throughout history. But it, too, fails to take in critical periods of development; that is, should we not ask ourselves when a child is *ready* for training. Even more important, it fails to take into account the tremendous advantage of positive training through the use of reinforcement.

Discipline, as it is commonly thought of, is largely a negative or aversive process aimed at eradicating so-called antisocial behaviors. One set of parents regularly spanked their fourteen-month-old daughter for screaming and angrily crying because they felt that if they allowed her to continue screaming, she would do so as a habit for the rest of her life. If she had been five years old or even three, their analysis of the situation might have been accurate because the little girl could have subsituted for her screaming, by language communication in the form of spoken requests. Of course, the technique they selected for eradicating screaming left much to be desired for children of any age, for there is a fundamental contradiction about using aggression to teach a child not to be aggressive. A baby of fourteen months has no effective language with which to communicate her frustrations or otherwise solve her problems. Therefore, she screams when her survival needs are not being met in one form or another. For this reason, instead of disciplining a fourteen-month-old baby for screaming, it would be preferable to train the same child between two and five years of age to explain her problems and frustrations *verbally* to receptive parents and to reinforce her for this constructive behavior. If, at the same time, the parents felt that the program should include three-minute time-outs for screaming, well and good.

## What Should We Do About Toilet Training?

Most children become toilet trained between two and three years of age. It would seem that the small returns gained by training infants under twenty months are not worth the trouble; in fact, trying to impose on a baby (through training) a regular habit for which it is physiologically unready may cause him unnecessary anxiety, stress, and frustration. Some mothers view early toilet training as a matter of personal pride and triumph. If their baby boy or girl is "toilet trained" by fourteen months, the mother gets a wonderful ego lift when she tells her friends what an efficient mother she is and what a precocious child she has. Toilet training before twenty months is pointless because the baby's conscious control of the sphincter muscle involved in elimination has not matured sufficiently. Even after twenty months, there are considerable individual time differences with respect to onset of conscious muscular control, and the length of time it takes to develop.

With some exceptions, toilet training can take place quite routinely in an unemotional atmosphere if, between twenty and twenty-four months, the parents regularly place the infant on the potty after meals, particularly breakfast, and praise the child consistently every time he is successful.

## How Can One Best Deal With Bedwetting?

Bedwetting is usually a sign of both anxiety and of an indirect "getting back" at the parents. As with most psychosomatic symptoms, this in no way contradicts the possibility that the child may have a physiological predisposition in the form of lax sphincter control or other disorders. Thus, it can be seen that the payoff in bedwetting is to release anxiety and to annoy the parents. Therefore, if the anxiety can be released in another way and if the agression can become more open and direct, the bedwetting should decrease. However, some payoff will always remain and this has to be counteracted. The authors have discovered a reinforcement system which works quite well with bedwetters and it is known as "doubling up." The system works like this: The first night that a child is dry, he receives 5c. If he is dry the following night, the reinforcer becomes 10c. The third successive night he receives 20c, the fourth successive night 40c, the fifth consecutive night 80c, sixth successive night $1.60, and the seventh successive night $3.20. The eighth successive night he returns to a reinforcer of 5c, but rest assurred that if a child has achieved seven successive nights, the habit of dryness is well on the way of becoming established. Should the child break the continuity of successively dry nights by wetting the bed, the doubling up automatically ceases and the first night he is again dry he receives the initial nickel. This system of doubling up not only reinforces the child for being dry each night, but also reinforces the child for his *continuity* of dryness on successive nights. Sometimes the doubling up system of reinforcement will bring good results fairly quickly, but if the anxiety and aggression are very well established it may take some months of reinforcement *and* counseling to bring about a successful remission of the problem.

## Doubling Up as a Reinforcement Technique

The system of doubling up as described above can be used in a variety of situations wherever the continuity of performance is crucial to the learning situation. In addition to bedwetting, we have used it with a points system for increasing fluency in reading (by doubling up points for each successive flash card correctly read at high speed), establishing teeth cleaning as a habit, and for building other essential habits. One important facet of doubling up as a reinforcer is that it is a powerful weapon with which to break up existing negative habits or to build up desirable new ones. Although the authors have not tried it, one might even double up for nail biting with a reward of a quarter for the first long fingernail, fifty cents for the second, a dollar for the third, and so on; in order not to break the bank, each hand should be treated as a separate doubling-up proposition.

## Can I Train My Child in Speech and Language?

Yes, it is extremely beneficial to expose your child to as much experience with language as possible during the critical period of language development from birth to the age of four years. Although speech in the form of very limited two-way communication does not really begin until between twelve and eighteen months, stimulating the child with constant exposure to language in those early months will lay a firm foundation for good articulation and an understanding of speech in succeeding years. Language development illustrates the "critical period" principal very clearly, because a child has acquired all the basic elements of adult language by the age of four years, even though, of course, much elaboration and vocabulary building must subsequently follow. It is self-evident that almost all children learn to speak their native language at an early age through an informal training and through circumstantial reinforcements. It is important to a child's healthy development that he is positively reinforced with smiles, laughter, pleasantries, and the like so that he comes to associate language with these enjoyable aspects of life. This will help him later in his schooling and in his linguistic relationships with other people. If his main exposure to language has been largely negative, abusive, and associated with punishment, especially from adults, he or she is likely to reject academic learning and to look on reading and related subjects as unnecessary chores.

## How Can I Prevent My Child From Being Spoiled?

Many parents are concerned about "spoiling" their children. They say, "But if I *give in* to my child he will be spoiled," and "If he *gets his own way* he'll soon be unmanageable." In these families, almost every request the child makes is regarded as a *challenge* to parental authority and so the request has to be denied. The problem of "spoiling" a child is so widespread that it calls for a detailed answer which itself must be divided into various age groupings.

The first group are the babies and toddlers under twenty months. *All mothers and fathers should realize it is impossible to "spoil" a baby between birth and twenty months.* Just the other day, we spoke to a mother who slaps her ten-month-old daughter for standing up in the high chair because otherwise she will become "spoiled." This is quite a common attitude amongst mothers of infants, and of course it is even more widespread as the children get older. *Babies and toddles who cannot yet speak reasonably fluently can only communicate by means of their actions, gestures and through noise such as laughing, crying, and screaming.* It is more than obvious that a baby of ten months or even eighteen months cannot say "I've had enough to eat, thank you, and please, may I get down from the table." In the authors' experience, babies and infants under two years of age should never be actively punished, especially physically. If any training is necessary (and try to make sure the child is physiologically and psychologically ready for training), it should be always very *positive* and if possible always involve much *social* reinforcement. If the foundations for an individual's later personality are laid down in the first two or three years of life, it is highly desirable that the infant is happy, full of laughter, very curious, enjoys physical contact, likes to eat, and bubbles with enthusiasm. By and large, babies and infants under twenty months or even two years of age should be given as much stimulation of all kinds (language, music, toys, places, people, and, providing the temperature is right, water). We have found and recommend to others that whenever behavior *management* is necessary in very young children, *distraction* is the key method. When Lynne, who is fourteen months old, eats her cereal in the morning, she sits in her high chair and plays with a great variety of objects and articles one at a time and almost invariably eats up all her food. Her favorite distraction is a box of artist's materials full of brushes, dry paints, trays, pencils, scraps of paper, and other odds and ends. If, during the day, Lynne is found playing with some tiny object which she might swallow or if she has found something she might damage, she is always given a harmless attractive substitute object *before* the "forbidden" one is removed. When babies and toddlers have tantrums as a reaction to their immense frustrations and inability to communicate, do not punish them or try to extinguish the tantrums with isolation or spanking. Usually, it is preferable to let the tantrum ride for a few moments to let the exasperation out and then try to distract them in some way. Of course, if it is at all possible to divine the cause of the frustration and if the need is a legitimate one (and almost all a baby's needs are legitimate), then resolve the tantrum by giving the baby what he wants or letting him do what he wants to do. This is not "giving in" because he was not forbidden anything in the first place. Lynne enjoys doing many things and has many well-established habits because we praise her, cuddle her a lot, and generally postively reinforce her for doing everything she can. Far from being restrictive, we are enthusiastic about Lynne experiencing and learning as much as possible.

Once communicative language enters into the picture and true social relationships begin to build with other children (usually from twenty months to two years onwards), the pattern of mainly positive training alters slightly. For Robin, our son, the last two years between two and four years of age have been rather hectic. Robin has been learning through reinforcement, discussion, imitiation, and role playing that the most effective way to overcome frustration is to find ways and means of solving the frustrating problem which is immediately disorganizing his life and making him angry. He most often gets angry because he cannot accomplish some act such as putting on his shirt or trying to make a siphon work properly in his bath. Rather than actually solve the problem in question for Robin, we may demonstrate it or role play the solution. Often we give advice or, at the most, help him over the crucial difficulties. When he does solve problems either by himself or with help, Robin is praised and his efforts applauded. Kate, who is seven years of age, has long since developed out of the tantrum stage even though she can still (and usually rightfully) exhibit irritation when frustrated. However, Kate's problem-solving ability is well advanced and this enables her to handle many situations to which she would otherwise react in an overemotional way.

As has been said in previous chapters, all children will be far more amenable to both positive and negative reinforcement training if they receive a generous amount of direct, personal *affection*. Little Lynne is always fractious unless she receives each day several ten-minute periods of cuddling, carrying, and physical romping. Although the older children can get by with a little less, if they are to be happy they too have to receive their quota of direct love.

## What Should I Do About Sexual Development and Masturbation in Children?

A graduate student who was in charge of a children's cottage once asked in a seminar what she should do about a twelve-year-old boy who masturbated frequently and openly in the bathroom in front of other children. Immediately, most of the other graduate students present suggested extinguishing his sexual behavior and began devising all kinds of programs to do so. We wished the students a lot of luck, adding that if they managed to extinguish the boy's sexual behavior they would have made a breakthrough which had never been achieved in the history of the human race. The students saw the point and eventually suggested direct counseling which would encourage the lad to masturbate in private like everybody else.

There are many people around who still look on sexual activity as shameful, dirty, or "unnecessary." In our experience, it is a rare parent who, on seeing little Johnny fondling his penis, does not automatically tell him to stop or finds some way of distracting him so that he stops. Children's sexual explorations of each other, masturbation, and any other childhood sexual activities are *perfectly natural* and are one aspect of healthy psychological development. Of course, all children should receive a full sex education in *both* the home and school from the time they first learn to speak. All sexual questions at any age should be answered openly and freely. If questions are *not* being asked about sex, then a "conspiracy of silence" is operating and the parents should investigate in themselves what is causing this damaging silence.

From puberty onward masturbation and petting are normal sexual outlets for the very powerful sexual drive. It is strange that for many people sexuality is a forbidden function during adolescence at the very time when evolution programed it to be at its most powerful. Perhaps the best way to counsel teenagers about sexuality is to point out that it carries with it a tremendous *responsibility,* especially to any babies which might be born outside marriage. In other words, sex is presented as a delightful, enriching, simple experience which is *not* dirty, shameful, or disgusting; however, to have a baby which will be born into a world with no home, no financial support, and no normal family relationships is a highly irresponsible act toward that baby. Therefore, it is pointed out, conception must not happen. The horns of the dilemma are only too obvious; on the one hand we have a tremendously powerful drive which will not be denied and on the other we have the possibility of conception. The only practical answer, and it is one which is already universally used, is masturbation and petting through to orgasm without intercourse. Otherwise, contraceptives must be recommended. At least this gives some preparation for sexuality in marriage, an area where undifferentiated sexuality in people over the last two hundred years has caused much conflict and bitterness between husbands and wives.

All children should read Dr. Sol Gordon's book on sex for

children entitled *Facts about Sex,* and all children of twelve or thirteen years of age should be given Dr. David Rueben's book, *Everything You Always Wanted to Know about Sex.* If sexuality, nudity, menstruation, defecation, and urination are always treated as healthy matters for open discussion by parents and children of any age, there will be few conflicts or problems arising from them during adolescence and in later years.

## How Can Anxiety and Fear Be Handled?

Almost all species seem to have fear in their makeup, and this is because it has tremendous survival value for each species. In the human race, fear is largely unprogramed, probably because of the multiplicity of environments in which children are raised. Eskimo children must learn to fear seawater as instant death, but Polynesians have to learn to swim in water like proverbial fish. City children have to acquire a healthy respect for motor traffic when crossing the road, while country children have to beware of getting too close to agricultural machinery.

Because we can so easily learn to fear objects or concepts, it is essential for every parent and teacher to take a long hard look at each one before he or she deliberately or unwittingly teaches children to be afraid of something.

Here is a list of some of the objects or concepts of which parents, teachers, or the community sometimes make children afraid: animals, spiders, nakedness, thunder and lightning, electricity, authority figures, climbing, reading, certain foods (including religious taboos), flying, some foreigners (especially so-called enemies), swimming, deep water, certain sports, mathematics, Shakespeare, leaving home, coming home, punishment, sunshine, rain, colds, aggression, getting messy, sexual organs, sexual acts, the opposite sex, pornography, alcohol, drugs, failure, success, work, leisure, marriage, loneliness, cruelty, touching, police, fire, fantasy, creativity, children, wealth, poverty, accidents, dentists, doctors, and death. A proportion of these fears may be legitimate and even quite valuable, but none of them should be instilled in a child to the point where they cripple development, hinder action, or prevent other learning. It is up to each person to decide which of the above list (and any others which may not have been included) are useful to the child and which might be a burden. In our experience, the *fewer* the fears with which a child is encumbered, the more secure and mature is his personal development through life. To possess a few mild *reality-based* fears is probably best, especially if they are combined with sound, rational scientific information concerning the survival value of each to the individual. For example, children should have a healthy respect for electricity but they should also have a detailed knowledge of how it works and how they can handle it efficiently in everyday life.

Fears are learned just as anything else is learned, on the principles outlined in previous chapters. Fears can be inculcated by positive or negative reinforcement, through imitation, by role playing, and even by physical positioning. Very often, the learning is circumstantial or imitative and parents usually pass on to their children their own fears by such unintentional means. It should be noted that the fears being referred to in this section include anxieties, misgivings, dislikes, awe, panic, terror, phobias, taboos, subservience, hatred, disgust, guilt, cowardice, foolhardiness, and plain naked fear itself.

### Desensitization

If a child (or adult) has already acquired or learned a specific deep-seated fear, then it may be possible to remove that fear, or at least reduce it, by a process of desensitization. When we are afraid we are always afraid of *something*—an object, a person, a group, a situation, an environment, or even the unknown.

Desensitization is a process of *unlearning* a fear. One desensitization technique is to reinforce a person every time he gets closer to the thing of which he is afraid. These movements toward a feared object, person, and so on, are often called "just noticeable differences" (or JND's), especially when the "movement" is just detectable. Of course, the movement may be in terms of time instead of miles, feet, and inches. For example, a person who is afraid of the dark may decide to stay in a dark room increasing the time by a JND of one minute each night. An example of a JND in distance might be a child who is afraid of cats. Each time he gets one foot closer to the cat he is reinforced. Eventually, the JND's may become the number of strokes of the cat's fur which the child makes.

School phobias in children may be as much a fear of leaving the security of mother and home as a fear of expecting terrible things to happen to them at school. If the exact object, subjects, or persons feared (including other children and the teacher) are known, then a desensitization program can be organized.

Note that in not a few cases the fear may be a *real* one. In such cases, the feared object will have to be removed from the environment. If a child fears a bully at school, something must be done to stop the bully from frightening the child in question. An intervener must be very careful to establish how real or "imaginary" a feared object or person is.

Some fears are generalization from one instance. A child receives an electric shock from a toaster and thereafter will never use one. Another child has a punitive teacher in first grade and never again likes school even though subsequent teachers may be kindly.

## What Can Be Done About Agression?

This is a topic which calls for a book in its own right, let alone one section of one chapter. Even so, a few pertinent points can be made. First of all, it is important to realize that like fear, aggression is largely the result of a training that may be partly circumstantial and partly deliberate. Once it is realized that aggressive habits are trained in children by parents and teachers, several points become clear. If adults shout at children, then by imitation those children will learn to shout. If adults abuse children, those children will learn to be abusive. If adults are impolite to children, those children will learn to be impolite. If adults hit and spank children, then those children will learn to hit and spank.

By the same learning token, children can be trained to be quiet, polite, and friendly. In other words, children learn to act and speak by observing the example of how others act and speak; they learn little by listening to admonitions from adults who do not practice what they preach. One is reminded of the old joke in which a mother was observed spanking her child and shouting "My God, I'll teach you to hit people, swear, and blaspheme, you little bastard." Please do not get the idea that there should be nothing negative in the child's environment. It has already been suggested several times that approximately 10 percent of the training of a child should involve negative reinforcement. The crucial point to be made is that the environment at home and school should be almost entirely positive, encouraging, and happy. *Negative reinforcement must never be abusive.*

If children fight with each other, throw tantrums, or resort to other kinds of physical violence, it is a psychological contradiction to hit them (spanking) as a punishment. It is much better to put the child or children in time-out (separately) for five or ten minutes and counsel one or other of the children each time.

Children who squabble a lot can be dealt with positively in two ways. First, they can be encouraged to try to settle their differences through discussion or even through a *formula*. An example of a formula would be for each to use the toy in question for five minutes in succession. The second much more effective technique is to reinforce the children positively for any behavior which is the direct counterpart or squabbling or fighting. For example, if the children are on a points system, then every ten minutes (or half hour) that goes by in a friendly atmosphere is reinforced by awarding them a predetermined number of points. In addition, any observed instance of *sharing* is reinforced immediately with a given number of points. Friendliness and sharing are the opposites of abuse and acquisitiveness, and a program of positive reinforcement for the former two and negative reinforcement for the latter two should soon bring about changes in behavior. Many parents and teachers are unpracticed at observing specific positive behaviors such as acts of friendliness and sharing, but these behaviors do occur and they are both observable and trainable. Sharing, in particular, is susceptible to role playing, particularly if reinforcement is given as a part of the role playing. Once again, praise is extremely important because it builds a pride in being thought of as a kind person and one who always shares. This training should start at an early age because even a three-year-old can be proud of being known as a "sharer" and a "kind boy."

Children over the age of *four years* who continue to have violent tantrums should also be programed with both negative and positive reinforcers. The way to extinguish tantrums is to put the child into time-out until he is reasonably quiet. The mother of the child who is in time-out must check with him every five minutes or sooner to ask him if he is ready to come out, allowing him to do so if he is ready. Should he then immediately become violently angry again, he goes straight back inside for another five minutes. At the same time as this negative reinforcement program is in operation, it is very advisable to begin teaching the child how to handle frustrating situations in a more mature fashion. It should be pointed out to him that getting very angry does not solve his immediate problem. Be sure that as a parent you do not directly solve his frustrating problem for him when he has a tantrum or you are merely reinforcing those tantrums. Encourage him to *discuss* his problems and then *help him to find a sensible solution.* Reinforce him with points every time he is frustrated but does not throw a tantrum. As a parent, check your own handling of the child to insure that the tantrums are not triggered by your own management systems. In all this, remember that while tantrums are normal reactions to frustrations in babies and toddlers, language and intelligence were given to children and adults to help resolve problems in a mature way.

## Is "Setting Limits" Important?

In our experience, the setting of limits for children is extremely important, just as it is for all society. As is the case with adults, children should know that there are regulations and laws which, if transgressed, will bring about fixed punishments. The unruly child who dominates the home, who is out of control, or who merely "gets away with it," is usually not only a source of misery at home, but also a problem in the school and the wider community.

There are two types of children who tend to "run wild" to the point of overdominating others in their environment. One is the child who is rarely reinforced either positively or negatively and who also receives very little direct attention from his parents. This surrounding parental weakness, which is found in many "liberal-minded" people, sets few limits and so the child grows up using those around him with little sense of personal responsibility, with few standards of social behavior, and with no thought of contributing to society in a constructive way. Such children should have had limits set for them from two years of age onwards. The second type of child who is unruly is usually labeled "psychopathic." The psychopathic child also has few standards of behavior and he is usually cruel and violent. Some textbooks describe these children as "emotionally frozen." They often live in families where punishment is frequent and severe, and the atmosphere very negative. It is not uncommon to find that these ruthless children have been spanked almost every day of their lives and that their parents gave them no love because love "would spoil them." Colin was one of these overpunished boys from a loveless family. He used to go around searching out babies whose mothers had left them for a moment or two outside shops in their baby carriages. Colin would scratch the babies' faces and dump them on the sidewalk before running from the scene as fast as he could. Thus, Colin's only revenge was to attack those who were harmless because it was far too dangerous to attack the true source of his problem—his parents. Colin also stole frequently, was extremely abusive, and was always fighting and quarreling with other children.

Once again, the answer is not the traditional one of liberalism or of strong discipline. It is a carefully considered program of positive training involving a high proportion of positive reinforcement for positive behaviors and (once a sound behavior-modification system is operating) some 10 percent negative reinforcement for unacceptable behaviors. Every home and classroom, if it is to work smoothly, must have some simple *rules and regulations* which children must abide by. These provide the limits within which the children's behavior must fall. If their behavior transgresses those limits, then the negative reinforcement programs must come into effect. (It is being taken for granted that the very strong positive reinforcement program is also in effect.) Be sure that the negative reinforcement is immediately contingent upon the negative act.

Within the limits sets (and they must be as carefully defined as in the law of the land), the child should have a considerable degree of personal freedom to choose his own activities and to make his own decisions. As he moves into adolescence, he should be given more and more freedom from the family and at the same time increasingly come under the limits set by society. If a youth or adolescent girl wants to change those limits and laws, encourage legal protest, for positive change is what life is all about; we would still live in caves if we did exactly as our parents did for generation after generation.

## What About the Child Who Doesn't Care?

Any person who "doesn't care" is stating his own diagnosis. He or she "doesn't care" because in the past he has been given no reason to value affection or other forms of positive reinforcement and because he has no regard for the negative reinforcements used to set limits, if indeed limits have been set. Ideally, the "don't care" type of child should never have been allowed to develop that way. Children who have been predominantly praised, loved, encouraged, and helped from birth and who have also been punished in mild ways from two years of age will never develop into "don't care" children. In the case of an older child who is already a "don't care" child, the best recourse is to search out those things which he himself values most, such as toys, money, candy, or viewing television. These can then be used in combination with a points system to positively reinforce desirable behaviors. He should also be praised, though at first not too effusively, whenever he is reinforced with points. Once the reinforcement program is instituted, try not to get tangled up in verbal battles with these children and ignore temporary breakdowns as it may take a little while to establish the program. In serious cases, professional counseling on behavior modification may be necessary. In the case of Colin, it was two years before he was able to say to his teacher-therapist, "I really do believe you like me." With most children, the development of "caring" about others, and the development of *a strong attachment to a sympathetic adult* occurs much sooner than two years; usually it is only a matter of weeks.

## What About Spanking?

The best answer we have ever heard to this query is that of a very experienced child psychiatrist who once said, "If you know of no other ways in which to handle your children's behavior then spanking it has to be." In our experience, looking at child rearing in its present state of "what is" rather than the idealistic "what should be," it would seem that most children are going to get spanked at least a few times in their lives, especially when they take the testing of limits and punishments as far as they will go. If Johnny, after careful counseling and after having put in time-out for five or ten minutes, promptly tears several books to shreds, a good spanking lets him know he has gone too far and that his indirect aggression is unacceptable. Of course, it is assumed here that Johnny is already receiving a fair amount of love, attention, and positive training with positive reinforcements. If Johnny is allowed to tear up books without limits being set, and after other punishments have been tried and found ineffective, then book tearing will become one of his standard negative aggressive outlets. This outlet is a very immature one and it should be explained to Johnny after the spanking that he is always free to talk over his angry feelings in an angry (but not abusive) voice in order to try and straighten out his problem. This discussion should be accepted by his mother and father.

We have found that on the *rare* occasions that spanking is necessary in order to set limits, the spanking should be swift, intense, and produce crying. It should de done only with the hand (never use a belt or other weapon) and it should be accompanied by clear statements as to why a spanking is being given. Always have the child repeat back several times the reason why he is being spanked and why the misdemeanor is antisocial or dangerous. Another good practice is to pair the spanking both before and afterwards with a finger tapping on the top of the forehead so that this can be used as a warning signal on later occasions and in circumstances where punishment of any kind is difficult—for example, in a supermarket. Robin, at age four, was already so conditioned to finger tapping as a cue that on one occasion when he had managed to cover most of the bathroom in black paint, he inquired very anxiously, "Arc you going to tap my head?" Already for him, this was the ultimate disgrace.

Once a child of three or four years has had limits thoroughly established, brief time-outs or even "waiting a minute" and light finger tapping are sufficient for behavior management purposes. Certainly, a well-loved, positively trained child with many legitimate outlets for his drives should need spanking very rarely, *if at all.* If anyone has to spank a child on average more frequently than once a month (an absolute maximum), then something is seriously wrong with the home behavior-management program. It is perhaps necessary at this point to say to the idealists in child rearing that theoretically, spanking small children of three years of age and over who can talk fluently (children under three years should never be spanked) should be completely unnecessary. However, to be practical, we know of only one pair of parents in that perfect category who raised their children to be extremely capable, mature individuals without any physical punishment.

The idealistic goal of attaining near-perfect behavior in children (and as a result in adults) and the idealistic technique of raising children in some kind of completely nonaggressive, all-loving, dutiful, gentle, totally enriching home environment is clung to by large numbers of parents, professional child workers, and some teachers who have genuine altruistic feelings but who are constantly frustrated because very few children or people measure up to the requirements of the ideals. We wish to go on record as fully accepting these ideals as an ultimate far-off goal and one which we should all ultimately work toward; we do not doubt that one day the meek, the peace lovers, and those of us who value life and living things will one day inherit the earth. But in the meantime, we have to devise realistic techniques and methods which will inch us towards that goal in very *practical* ways, and the obvious and natural place to start is in the home and the school. If we are to reduce the number of psychopaths and irresponsible freewheelers in our community, we have to institute behavior-management programs in all our homes and schools which will train children not only to respect our social limits, rules, and regulations but also have a compassion for the needs of others and a wish to build and contribute to a healthy home and community life.

## Is Creativity Learned?

Creativity has already been mentioned in several sections previously, but it is so important that it warrants a section to itself. The short answer to the above question is yes. If a child is praised and reinforced for producing, acting, or performing creatively in any area of life, he *learns* to enjoy that creative activity. This is true whether or not the child has a real talent in that subject area. Many people who enjoy painting or music and who are creative in those fields obviously do not possess the genius of a Leonardo, Picasso, Beethoven, or Stravinsky, but each has something to contribute to the general benefit of us all. As aspects of creativity, both originality and ingenuity can also be praised and otherwise reinforced, always provided the adults involved recognize true creativity when they see it. In conversations with numerous (and some famous) creative people, the authors have all too often had related to them dismaying accounts of how orthodox teachers, clergymen, and parents did their utmost to pressure individual attempts at creativity into the standard mold of conformity. Unfortunately, most people fear creative innovation in others, for it threatens to shatter the platform of security they have so carefully built throughout life. Many parents and teachers raise their children on the principles of "Thou shalt conform, do as I do, act as I act, believe what I believe, and accept what I say without too many questions." Then when those same children reach maturity, their parents say "Go forth, be fruitful, be creative, and lead a full rich life." The inherent contradiction is not recognized or understood.

Once it is realized, innate talent apart, that creativity and originality are *learned* by children (though sometimes they may be the result of a reaction against authority) we have a neat synthesis to replace the traditional viewpoint that creativity and training are antagonistic. There is no contradiction in training children to respect the rights and property of others and in training them to be "liberated" creative individuals. Most great philosophers have had as one of their themes the compatibility of human dignity with creative individuality.

Therefore, while we should positively reinforce creativity and originality as well as conformity to all those reasonable rules and regulations which contribute to harmonious human relationships, we should always strive to make a clear distinction between creative, original contributions to life and individualistic antisocial acts and behaviors which threaten to break the constructive forces in our society or which may impede its social evolution. This is an extremely difficult discriminant task. Many of our greatest geniuses including Socrates, Christ, Galileo, Gandhi, not to mention numerous great statesmen and scientists, were all incarcerated or eliminated for being creative. *Life is a process of change and most people in their search for security and stability fail to see that process. Today,* just as yesterday most of us do not see ourselves or our institutions as creative agents or instruments of change. Orthodoxy, dogma, and traditional viewpoints still continue to condemn all kinds of creative and constructive innovators. Too many people, fearing the new, suggest old solutions to new problems. How often do we hear "All he needs is a few good hard spankings and that will set him straight," or "If everyone went to church like me and believed, society would be well," or "The poor are just lazy and if they will not help themselves no one else should." Social problems, family problems, and even environmental problems call for new creative solutions rather than one-sentence clichés from the past; our children have to learn how to search creatively for new answers and fresh solutions.

## Can Problem Solving Be Learned?

Creating new solutions to our problems calls for a new approach in both home and school as to how children are trained to solve problems. The conventional school system and home teaches children to be passive, accepting, believing, and to dislike problem solving because it is so boring. Yet, man's brain is primarily a problem-solving machine because successful problem solving has tremendous survival value for the human species. The curricula of all schools should be changed to be a very active one in which the central theme is always creative problem solving. All children who successfully learn to problem solve or who even attempt to find new solutions must be reinforced for their effort. If, with some help, little Johnny discovers that three times six is the same as six plus six plus six, then he should be positively reinforced for his discovery. If a group of children can work out how to measure rainfall and actually do it, they are participating in a creative discovery. This is by no means a new idea. Philosophers and educators for centuries have advocated that children learn through personal discovery and active problem solving, preferably with lots of equipment. Unfortunately, universities demand that their students pass examinations. And therefore, high schools, junior high schools, and elementary schools usually follow suit. This mania for passing examinations immediately causes the curricula to become very formalized, and learning becomes a cramming process on the part of the teacher and a passive, rather boring assimilation on the part of students. The detailed solution to these problems is a complex one and is not the major topic of this book. However, if teachers and parents begin to reinforce their children for creative problem solving it will go a long way toward solving creatively the numerous problems of our present-day society and its educational systems.

# REFERENCES AND BIBLIOGRAPHY

Bannatyne, Alexander: *Psycholinguistic Color System of Reading, Writing, Spelling and Language.* Rantoul, Ill., Learning Systems ities. Springfield, Thomas, 1971.

Bannatyne, Alexander: *Language, Reading and Learning Disabil-* Press, 1970. (P.O. Box 909, 61866.)

Bannatyne, Alexander and Bannatyne, Maryl: *Motivation Management Materials (for the elementary classroom).* South Miami, Fla., Kismet Publishing Co., 1970. (P.O. Box 90, 33143.)

Bannatyne, Alexander and Bannatyne, Maryl: *Home Behavior Management Charts for Children.* South Miami, Fla., Kismet Publishing Co., 1970. (P.O. Box 90, 33143.)

Bannatyne, Maryl and Bannatyne, Alexander: *Body Image/Communication. A Psycho-Physical Development Program.* Rantoul, Ill., Learning Systems Press, 1972. (P.O. Box 909, 61866.)

Bijou, Sidney and Baer, Donald: *Child Development I.* New York, Appleton-Century-Crofts, 1961.

Ferster, C.B.: *Arbitrary and Natural Reinforcement.* In published proceedings, 1967 International Convocation on Children and Young Adults with Learning Disabilities, Pittsburgh, Pa., 1967.

Gordon, Sol: *Facts about Sex, A Basic Guide.* New York, John Day, 1969, 1970. (257 Park Avenue South, 10010.)

Madsen, Charles and Madsen, Cliff: *Teaching Discipline.* Boston, Allyn and Bacon, 1970.

Millenson, J.R.: *Principles of Behavioral Analysis.* New York, Macmillan, 1967.

Patterson, G.R. and Gullion, M.E.: *Living With Children: New Methods for Parents and Teachers.* Champaign, Ill., Research Press, (P.O. Box 2459, Sta. A, 61820.)

Reuben, David: *Everything You Always Wanted to Know About Sex.* New York, David McKay, 1969. (750 Third Avenue, 10017.)

*APPENDIX*

# A LIST OF REINFORCERS
# FOR HOME AND SCHOOL

Note that some of the following reinforcers are suitable for use with children at home and some for use with children at school, but most can be adapted to either behavior setting. Many of the reinforcers listed have been taken from the authors' publications, *Motivation Management Materials* and *Home Behavior Management Charts* (see references). The order of the list is in no way intended to imply that some reinforcers are better than others. Programs must be devised for each group or each individual in a specific behavior setting. The reinforcers given below are not mutually exclusive and several may be used for a variety of purposes with each group or individual child.

*Token Reinforcers*

Plastic tokens or coins.
Points on a chart.
Points in an account book.
"Toy" paper money.
Real money.

*Symbolic Reinforcers*

Colored shiny stars or seals.
Pictorial rubber stamps (e.g. flag).
Verbal rubber stamps (e.g. VERY GOOD WORK).
Badges of achievement or responsibility (as in the Boy Scouts or services).

*Verbal (Social) Reinforcers*

Good boy or girl (adding the name of the child strengthens any

110

verbal reinforcement).

Good (fine, excellent, wonderful, neat, quick, etc.) work.

Isn't John wonderful the way he always shares his things with his little sister.

Mary is the best helper in this town; we are proud of her.

David loves to give things to people; he's so generous.

Joan takes great care with her work; she loves to get it right.

What a good (helper, worker, sharer, cleaner, etc.) you are.

How quietly (happily, contentedly, etc.) you two children play together.

What a happy (industrious, cheerful, honest, etc.) child you are.

Your are so *right* always to tell the truth.

### Privileges

Additional TV time (usually one extra half hour after usual bed-time).

Special outings such as lunch or dinner out or visits, bowling, zoo, picnics, etc.

Free choice time (20 minutes in school).

Using equipment such as slide viewer, 3-D viewers, filmstrip viewers, or even film projectors.

### Adult Participation Activities

Story reading.

Table games (e.g. playing cards, Monopoly, bingo, checkers, chess, Scrabble®, etc.).

### Collecting (*Each time give one object for several points*)

Postage stamps.

Shells.

Gummed picture seals.

Plastic or metal miniatures (cars, Indians, soldiers, animals, etc.).

Doll's clothing (Dawn, Barbie, etc.).

Shells, rocks, minerals (for older children).

Comic books (good quality).

Records.

Coins.

*Special Games (Earned time—these may also be adult participation)*

Bumper pool or regular pool.
Slot car racing.
Table tennis.

*Special Educational Activities (Group or individual)*

Oil, acrylic, or tempora painting.
Film/Drama.
Workshop.
Sports.
Dancing (all kinds).
Sculpture (large).
Murals (large).
Pottery (with wheel).
Gardening.
Band/Group/Orchestra.
Craft (weaving, etc.).
Fashion clothes.
Zoo.
Museum of artifacts.
Newspaper publication.
Photography.
Cheer leading.
Constructional toys (kit sets, erector sets, Leggo, etc.).
Gymnastics.
Puppets and theater dioramas.

*Social Activities*

Parties (classroom or home).
Group games (relays, etc.).
Watching movies (home, school, or theater).
Playing grown-up.
 Shopkeeping.
 House.
 Hospitals (first aid, nursing, etc.).
 Post office (letter writing, mailing, etc.).
 Airport (travel tickets, etc.).
 Tableau dressing up in costumes.

Group projects (medieval castle, dairy farm, airport, racetrack, etc.).

*Food and Drink*

Small candies, raisins, nuts, cereal.
Cookies (in pieces or whole).
Coke®, Pepsi®, Seven-up®, etc.

*"Presents" for Points*

Children on a points system may wish to save up several hundreds or even thousands of points for objects such as the following:
Record player and records.
Drums or musical instrument such as guitar.
New bike.
Cassette recorder.
Walkie-talkie.
Own television set.
Transistor radio.
Large, expensive toys.
Camera.

*Junior High and High School*

At this level, the teaching staff can award the school equivalent of trading stamps which the students stick in books. They may earn many of the above items, but the most desirable one (from an informal survey) would be a contract to use the stamps to earn Friday afternoon off on a minute-by-minute basis.

*Remember . . .*

Whenever possible, any material or primary reinforcers should always be accompanied by praise, caressing, and recognition reinforcement. The human positive attachment relationship is a major key to maturation.

# INDEX

115